1979

Merry Christmas, Louise

I hope this book will give

you hours of pleasure in the years

to come.

Love, Mama

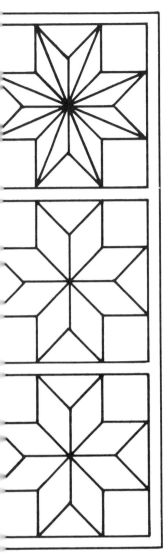

YANKEE HOME CRAFTS

by Barbara Radcliffe Rogers

Drawings by Ray Maher

YANKEE, INC., Dublin, New Hampshire

This book has been prepared
by the staff of Yankee, Inc.

Designed by Carl F. Kirkpatrick

First Edition

Copyright 1979, by Yankee, Inc.
Printed in the United States of America

Library of Congress Catalog Card No. 78-66324
ISBN 0-911658-85-8

To my father, who would have liked it.

Table of Contents

Foreword

The crafts and skills of times past have always fascinated me. From the homey and primitive cornhusk dolls to priceless pieces of the quilter's art, they hold a fascination that is as much in the way of life they represent as in the craft itself.

Learning an almost forgotten skill and teaching it to someone else makes us somehow kin to the men and women who have built our rich artistic heritage. And it keeps that heritage alive.

This book represents my own interests and, like me, it is a jack-of-all-trades, master of none. The reader will not become an expert in any of the skills just from reading this book. The projects explained are just a beginning. But after meeting them here, perhaps the reader will find one to continue studying and eventually master. I hope so.

Or, like me, perhaps the reader will enjoy a project here and there, trying his hand at a number of different skills. Either way, we are together carrying on a wonderful tradition of handwork.

Many people have instructed me in the crafts described here, and many have joined me in enjoying them. All deserve my thanks and a few deserve special mention. Of course my own family; my mother and father who taught me the basic skills of sewing, embroidery, metal and woodworking that I would later draw on; Tim, with whom I have shared so many of the projects, from tin cookie cutters to fake graining; and Julie who wants to learn skills far beyond her years and surprises us with her ability.

For the help of Jan Krise with the bronze stenciling, and Mary Ann Williams with theorem, the company of Pat Greene and Mickey Bertera in long evenings of quilting, and the encouragement and general knowledge of Dolores Kott in many areas of early handicraft, I am grateful.

A special note of thanks goes to the many craftsmen at Old Sturbridge Village who have patiently answered my endless questions as I learned. They provide one of the finest resources available on early 19th-century life in rural New England, and their personal interest in their work is an inspiration to the 20th-century world.

B.R.R.

Fig. 1-1

CHAPTER 1

Making Cornhusk Dolls and Doormats

Making Cornhusk Dolls and Doormats

Cornhusk Dolls

Whether it was the need for a craft material or the axiom of "waste not, want not" that brought about the first cornhusk dolls and doormats is hard to say. But the creative use of cornhusks has been with us a long time — a craft as native to America as corn itself.

There are as many ways to make old-fashioned cornhusk dolls as there are people making them, and nearly every method is authentic in that its roots can be traced to early New England, the Southern Appalachians, an Indian tribe, or other early habitation of America.

A cornhusk doll begins with ears of corn. Ordinary sweet cornhusks saved from the kitchen will make fine dolls. When you are shucking corn, save out the inner husks — the small, finer-grained ones nearest the cob. Lay these out on newspapers or screens in the sun, where they will bleach to a creamy oat color as they dry. They will curl and shrivel, but will smooth out again when you begin to work with them.

Save and dry some cornsilk, too — both the inner white silk and the outer brown tangled silk. These can serve as hair for your dolls.

When the husks are quite dry, they are ready to use. Now soak them for a few minutes in warm water to soften them and lay out on a towel. It is important to first dry, and then soak, although it may seem odd, because the initial drying causes the husk to assume a final size and shape, which the short soaking will not alter. Soaking merely makes the husks easier to work with and helps keep them from splitting.

Cornhusks used fresh will draw and curl as they dry, ruining the doll made from them; drying in a bundle (on the doll) instead of spread out separately on screens or newspapers is apt to cause mildew.

For a small doll, begin with six good husks (Fig. 1-2). Cut off the puckered part that attached to the base of the cob. Also cut off the tip of the pointed end, forming an almost rectangular piece, a little narrower at the top than at the bottom (Fig. 1-3).

Choose the two smoothest husks and put them together, one on top of the other like two sheets of paper. Then take two more, and place the smoother husks between them, making a sandwich — the smoother husks being the filling. Tie all four firmly about three-quarters of an inch from the top end (Fig. 1-4). Now reverse the bunch, so that the tied top is at the bottom, and peel down the strips of husk over the knot (as though you were peeling a banana) so that the bunch is turned inside out (Fig. 1-5). The knot will be on the inside, and the best husks on the outside. The top, with the knot inside, will be the head of the doll.

Use good sturdy cotton thread or string for tying. There is nothing so aggravating as to have the ties break after the doll is completed, which will happen if you use strips of husks for tying. The new synthetic threads are also unsuitable because they stretch.

As you turn the husks down over the knot, notice which is the very smoothest and turn it last, pulling it around the others to form a smooth face. The pucker in the top will be covered with hair, but the husk should be stretched around to form the chin. This is possible because of the slightly elastic nature of cornhusks — similar to crepe paper when stretched crosswise. Tie the neck securely. Now your doll has begun to take shape (Fig. 1-6).

Stephen T. Whitney Photo

Fig. 1-2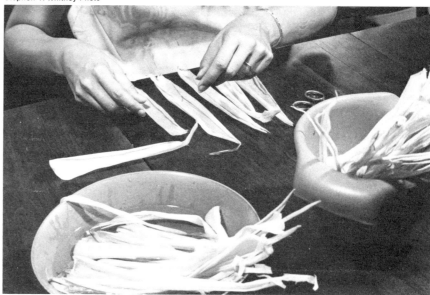

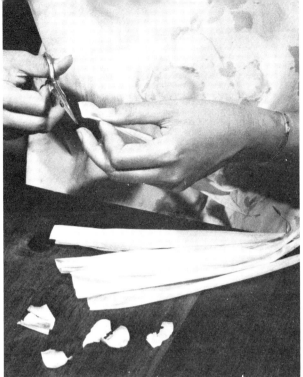

Fig. 1-3
Stephen T. Whitney Photo

Fig. 1-4
Stephen T. Whitney Photo

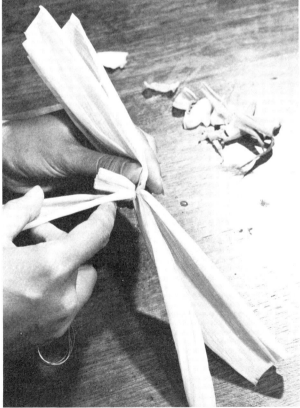

Fig. 1-5
Stephen T. Whitney Photo

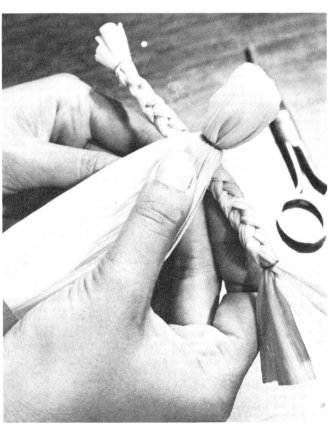

Fig. 1-6
Stephen T. Whitney Photo

Fig. 1-7

Fig. 1-8

Fig. 1-9

Fig. 1-10

Making Cornhusk Dolls and Doormats

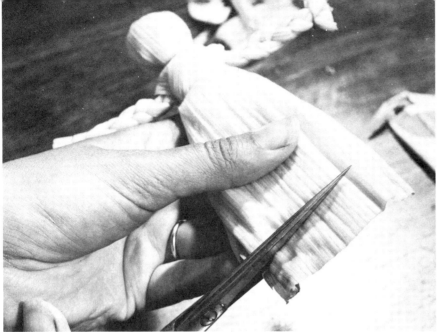

Fig. 1-11

Arms can be made by either rolling or braiding additional husks. For rolled arms, take one or two husks and roll with the "grain" lengthwise into a tight tube long enough for both arms. For braided arms, braid three cornhusks together tightly, tying at either end of the braid (Fig. 1-7). Finish by tying a strip of husk over the thread at each end of the braid (Fig. 1-12). Rolled arms do not require tying (see page 16 for a third type of cornhusk arm). Thread the arm piece through the middle of your doll, between the front and back husks and right under the tied neck (Fig. 1-6). Take two more husks and fold one over each shoulder, crossing them at the doll's waist (Fig. 1-8), and tie the waist (Fig. 1-9).

Now choose husks for the skirt, soak briefly and trim as before. You will need three or more husks, depending on how full a skirt you wish. For a doll with narrower hips, tie the husks on directly at the waist. Tie a narrow strip of wet cornhusk around the waist to cover the thread and husk ends. Let this strip dry before trimming the ends, or leave the ends long, like apron ties. For a puffier skirt, tie the skirt husks on to the waist upside down and peel them down over the waistband as you did when making the head (Fig. 1-10).

Trim the bottom of the skirt so that it is even; test by standing the doll up (Fig. 1-11). You may have to trim the skirt a bit more when the doll is completely dry.

The basic doll is now complete except for hair and additional trimming. To make hair, smooth white glue on the head with your finger (but not on the face!), take a tangle of dried cornsilk, and wrap around the doll's head, patting it down into the glue. You can use a tuft of lamb's wool or ravelled-out yarn instead of cornsilk.

A bonnet or hat is easily formed by wrapping a husk over the top of the head, exposing the face and front of the hair (Fig. 1-13). Fold it from each side towards the center of the back so that the folds meet at the back of the neck (Fig. 1-14). Tie with thread around the neck to

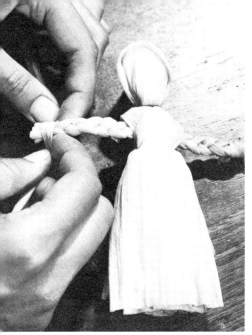

Fig. 1-12

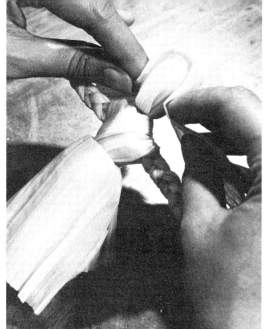

Fig. 1-13

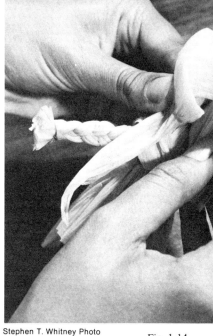

Fig. 1-14

secure the bonnet, then tie a strip of husk around the neck to hide the thread (Fig. 1-15). The ends of the bonnet husk can be trimmed neatly about a half inch below the tie.

The wet husks are pliable enough so that other types of head covering can be formed from them — turbans, cowls, veils, or even long cornhusk braids.

Having made the basic doll, you can vary her shape, stance and costume as you wish. While her arms are still damp, tie or wire them into the position you prefer (Fig. 1-16). When the doll is dry, remove the ties or wire, and the arms will remain in place.

A shawl is a strip of wet husk tucked under the arms after the doll has dried, or while the arms are tied into position and drying. An apron is made like a short skirt, then trimmed so that it covers the front of the skirt only. Tie a bow around the doll's neck, or give her a muffler.

As I mentioned earlier, there is another kind of arm you can make, although it is best to make your first doll with the braided or rolled arms already described. The trouble is that braided arms look braided, and rolled arms do not hold their shape well. A more lifelike arm is the wrapped arm, which has hands that will actually hold things, such as a broom or basket handle.

Form two bundles of rolled husk into long loops, each the length of an arm. Tie the unlooped ends all together with thread. Then wrap the connected loops around with narrow strips of husk, leaving only a rounded loop for the hand showing at each end of the wrapped sleeve. Thread the wrapped arm through the middle of the doll, between the front and back husks before tying the waist, just as you did for the braided or rolled arm, and finish as before.

A fancy leg-o-mutton sleeve can be made using a wrapped or rolled

Making Cornhusk Dolls and Doormats

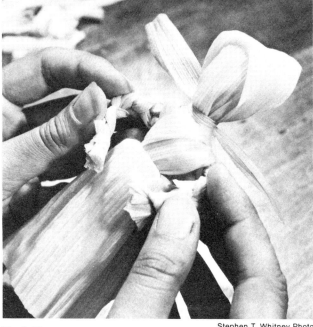

Fig. 1-15

Fig. 1-16

arm. Take a piece of husk and tie it on about one inch from one end of the arm, so that its long end extends well over the "hand" end of the arm. Pull the husk back over the tie so that the hand and lower arm are exposed and the tied-on husk forms a puffed sleeve. Tie in the center to secure (the tie will be hidden by the body of the doll), and repeat on the other end of the roll to form the other sleeve.

There is almost no limit to the accessories you can make for your dolls. An oblong garden basket can be formed from one husk with box-folded corners and a handle secured with a drop of glue. Tiny baskets can be woven or braided from strips of husk.

A flat Shaker sieve is made from a strip of husk doubled and bent into a ring, with a piece of cheesecloth glued over the bottom and trimmed. Or fashion a bread tray from an oval of balsa wood rimmed with braided husk. The bread is a tiny loaf made from a snip of real bread dough, formed into a braided or tapered loaf and baked crisp-hard in a slow oven.

A broom is simply a straight stick with a bundle of shredded husks tied on the bottom and trimmed even. Other implements can be carved from wood — butter churns, paddles, rakes, laundry sticks and tubs — your own imagination will suggest others.

Perhaps you have seen the modern cornhusk dolls sold in gift shops. Their heads are perfectly round, being formed over styrofoam balls or wooden beads, and their arms bend because they are wired through the center. These dolls are decorative, and will suggest ideas for your own experiments, but they are not authentic. The old-fashioned dolls perfected by our ancestors before styrofoam may take a bit more time to make, but they are authentic, and each finished doll will have its own special character — unlike the modern dolls which tend to a certain uniformity.

Making Cornhusk Dolls and Doormats

A Cornhusk Mat

To make a cornhusk doormat, you need about a bushel of husks (this doesn't take as many meals as you might expect) and a husk splitter. Take a piece of board about a foot long, and pound two thin nails clear through it so the points stick out the other side about an inch and a half apart. This is your splitter.

Fill an old wash tub with very hot water and put the husks in it. Cover to keep it warm. Let them soak until they are soft and easily worked, then draw each husk with the grain along the two nails. This will split the husks to give you pieces of even width. (Discard the narrow scraps or save them for other cornhusk projects.) It is possible to split dry husks, but since dry ones are curled and twisted, it is much easier to work with wet husks. When all are split, return them to the tub with more hot water.

Begin with three husks and cut them in different lengths. Cut just the pointed tip off one; make the second two-thirds the length of the first and the last one-third that length. These will be your starters; as you braid, they will end in different places.

Tie the small (tip) ends together tightly with good stout linen or heavy cotton thread. Don't use synthetics since they often stretch. Attach the tied ends to a braiding clamp if you have one, or to a clipboard, which you can then hold down with one foot.

Braid evenly, and when you come to within an inch of the butt (stem) end, pull the end up to stick out the top of the braid and begin

Paul A. Darling Photo

Fig. 1-17 *A cornhusk doormat photographed on exhibit at the South County Museum, North Kingstown, Rhode Island.*

Making Cornhusk Dolls and Doormats

braiding in another, tip end first. In this way, your braid will have regularly spaced scrapers sticking out of it which will eventually cover the surface of the finished mat.

Plan to finish the braiding the same day it is begun. If you leave the braiding for more than a few minutes, return all the braid to the tub of hot water. Be sure to keep the unused husks well covered by the water. Keep the braid firm, and as even as possible.

It will take about 12 feet of braided husks to make a square foot of mat, so you can judge accordingly. A small doormat would take about 30 feet of the braid. When you have a braid long enough for the size mat you wish to make, tie the end so it won't come undone as you sew.

Although your mat may be other shapes, the easiest to begin with is an oval. If the braid is not wet, soak it again. Fold the first two feet of the braid in half (do not cut the braid). Sew the two strips together, side by side, using a long heavy needle and stout linen thread. Sew firmly, but not so tightly that it puckers. Be sure not to twist the braid, since all the little stubby ends must be on the top.

This foot-long doubled piece is the center of your mat; the rest of the braid will be coiled and sewn around it. The size of this foundation determines the proportion of the finished mat. Its length is the difference between the length and width of the mat: a one-foot center foundation makes a mat one foot longer than it is wide. This is about right for a small doormat. A larger mat will be in better proportion if you start with an 18-inch or two-foot center.

Continue to stitch the remaining braid around in a flat coil until it is all used up. Keep the unsewn braid moist. Lay the braid alongside the mat on a flat surface as you work, taking care not to let it pull or twist and warp the mat. When you come to the end of the braid, untie it and stitch the three lengths into the edge of the mat so they taper smoothly.

Now dry the mat thoroughly. Depending on the weather, this could take as long as a week, but a day or two in the sun is usually sufficient.

When the mat is dry, take a three-tined cooking fork and draw the tines through each of the butt ends you left sticking out on top of the mat. This shreds them and gives the entire mat a coat of scratchy "fleece" that does the boot-wiping work.

The mat is now ready. Variations on the mat will occur to you. A plain mat without the shaggy butt ends can be made from the longer husks of field corn and would be suitable for a front door or an entry where mud and snow aren't so likely to be tracked in. (Just don't pull out the butt ends.)

The mat can be dyed a rich dark brown by soaking it in boiling water with butternut or black-walnut hulls.

A well-used and discolored mat can be refreshed in this way to cover stains as long as the mat itself is still in good condition. Wash the mat well with the strong spray from a garden hose, and submerge it in a washtub with boiling water and black-walnut or butternut hulls. These mats are sturdy and will endure years of heavy wear. ✸

CHAPTER 2

Bayberry Candles

The place of the candle in American life has changed since Colonial days. Once an absolute necessity, candles are now an elegant accessory. And candle-making, once a major project for the family each fall, is now both an enjoyable craft and a history lesson.

In the late fall when bayberries are ripe, the bay bushes (also known as wax myrtle) will be laden with gray berries. Several quarts of berries are needed to yield enough wax for one large candle. That may sound discouraging, but since bay usually grows over a wide area, any one location should provide you with ample berries. They pick faster if you rake them off in bunches with your fingers into a wide basket.

Back in the kitchen, pick over the berries, cover with water, and simmer very gently for an hour. Let the pot sit overnight in a cool place to harden the wax that will float to the top. Next morning, remove the disc of wax, picking off any sediment that may adhere to the bottom. Melt the wax in a little water, very slowly over low heat, and strain the mixture through a piece of muslin. Work in a warm place so the wax won't harden as it is being strained. If you have a lot of berries, work in small batches. Let cool overnight again, and in the morning remove and examine the wax disc.

If any sediment still remains in the wax, reheat the wax as above in the water, and strain a second time.

BE VERY CAREFUL WHILE WORKING WITH HOT WAX. Wax will burst into flame at a high temperature even if there is no flame near it. A woodstove is excellent for melting wax as the pan is

Fig. 2-1 *Poured candles can be made in old or new molds, but old ones should have dents removed before use.*

not set directly over the flame. Keep a cover for the pan handy so that you can smother the flames if the wax should ignite.

When the wax is perfectly clean, let it cool, and again lift the disc off the water when hard. Dry the wax and reheat (alone, without water, this time) to a temperature of 180° F. A double boiler or a crockpot makes a good vessel for melting wax safely.

From here on, the process differs depending on whether you have candle molds or intend to dip the candles.

Molds

Be sure the molds are clean inside and perfectly dry.

Cut candle wicking (not string!) longer than the mold, and insert the wick into the mold and through the hole in the bottom. This is easier if you dip just the very tip of the wicking in a little hot wax and let it harden first. (If too much of the wicking is dipped, it will be hard to knot the end.) Knot the wick on the outside of the hole to seal. Tie the top of the wick to a stick suspended along the top of the mold. Pour a little wax into the bottom of the mold and allow to harden.

Use a pitcher, teapot or watering can to pour the hot wax so that you can aim the flow directly into the mold. Before pouring, put the mold over a plate or other surface from which drippings may be scraped. These can be remelted and used.

Pour the wax down the side of the mold, so that air is forced out as the mold fills. Otherwise your candles will have air bubbles. The wax will shrink slightly as it hardens, so you should keep adding more to fill the mold completely.

Leave the mold in a cool place overnight. With the tip of a sharp knife, loosen the wax at the base of the mold and lift out the candles. If they stick, dip the molds very quickly into hot water to loosen the candles. If you do do this, be sure to hold the candles in the air until the outer layer is perfectly hard, or they will scar when you lay them down. You can trim the base with a sharp knife.

Dipping

To make dipped candles, you will need a container as deep as the candle will be tall. If you have only a little wax, the narrower your container, the longer the candle you can make.

The trick to dipping is to have the wax exactly the right temperature. Wax that is too cool will thicken and make dipping difficult; wax that is too hot will melt off the previous layer. The best temperature is 165°-170°F. If you don't have a deep-frying thermometer, you can experiment to find the right temperature.

Cut a wick twice the length of your candles plus three inches. Tie the wick over a long pencil or stick, looping it in two half-hitches so

A Handy Iron Pad

A handy ironing aid can be made from bayberries — you need only a handful or two. The wax in the berries makes an excellent coating to smooth the plate of an electric iron.

To make an iron pad, cut two equal rectangles of sturdy cotton fabric a little larger than the plate of your iron. Stitch them together firmly, right sides together, leaving a three-inch space unstitched for turning. Turn the pad inside out and fill loosely with bayberries. It should feel like an under-stuffed bean bag (Fig. 2-3).

Complete the pad by turning in the remaining raw edges and blind-stitching together. You can decorate it with a little ribbon in one corner, or a cotton eyelet ruffle stitched around the edges of the pad. Just don't use any synthetics that won't take all ironing temperatures, and don't put anything on the face of the pad.

To use, simply run the hot iron over the face of the pad a few times. The iron will then glide smoothly, and the room will be filled with the fragile scent of bayberries as you iron.

These make wonderful Christmas presents — original, pretty and useful.

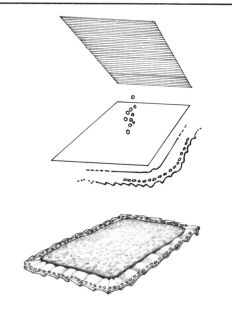

Fig. 2-2 *A handful of berries stitched between two layers of fabric makes an iron pad. Add a fancy edging for an attractive and practical gift.*

Fig. 2-3 *An Old Sturbridge Village "interpreter" dips bayberry candles by the half dozen into a wide pan. (Courtesy Old Sturbridge Village, Sturbridge, Massachusetts.)*

Old Sturbridge Village Photo

that the two ends hang down about two inches apart. If you have only enough wax for one candle, you can tie a single wick and dip in a very narrow container, or you can make two shorter candles rather than one long one.

Dip both the connected wicks into the hot wax at once, lift out, and hang until cool enough to touch. After the first dipping, pull each wick straight. Thereafter, the wax will keep your candles perfectly straight as the layers build up.

Continue dipping, letting the wax cool and dry between dippings until the candles reach the desired thickness. If you are making thin tapers, be sure that the finished tapers are thick enough to hold up without breaking and not burn down too fast.

When the candles are thick enough, let them harden overnight before trimming their bases with a sharp knife. It is customary to leave the candles in pairs until they are used.

A good way to present candles as a gift is to tie them together with a ribbon into which you have tied a sprig of bay leaves and berries, with a little note telling about the candles and how they were made — how many berries it took, for example, and whether they were dipped or made in an antique mold.

Once you have made candles, it is easy to tell why our forebears rose with the sun and retired early to bed. Light was a precious commodity!

CHAPTER

3

Apple-Head Dolls

Dried apples take on a wrinkled, leathery appearance that suggests the skin of elderly farmers, fishermen or others who have been exposed to wind and sun for many years. It was only natural that somewhere in history someone would have the idea of using a dried whole apple as a doll head.

There is some disagreement as to the origin of the doll: some sources credit the Iroquois Indians, others claim it was European. It is also quite likely that the idea may have begun in several different places. Whatever their origins, apple-head dolls became part of our American craft heritage very quickly. As in the case of cornhusk dolls, the materials are readily available, and most are free.

Although there are as many ways of making bodies for the dolls as there are doll makers, the heads are made in much the same way everywhere.

Use a firm dry apple — MacIntosh is too juicy, but Golden Delicious or other hard winter apple works well. Peel the apple, leaving stem and blossom and a little peeling around each. Rinse well in cold water and dry.

Using an orange stick or toothpick (not a steel knife blade), make a slit in the apple where you want the mouth to be. Turn the corners up or down or make the line straight, but make it deeper toward the center. The slit should be about 1/4-inch deep. Next make rounded slits at each corner of the mouth, surrounding it like a pair of parentheses (Fig. 3-2a).

I stop here, but many doll makers also make slits for the eyes and

Fig. 3-1 *A miniature crazy quilt is the finishing touch for this seated apple-head doll created by Allyn Lurgio of New Boston, New Hampshire.*

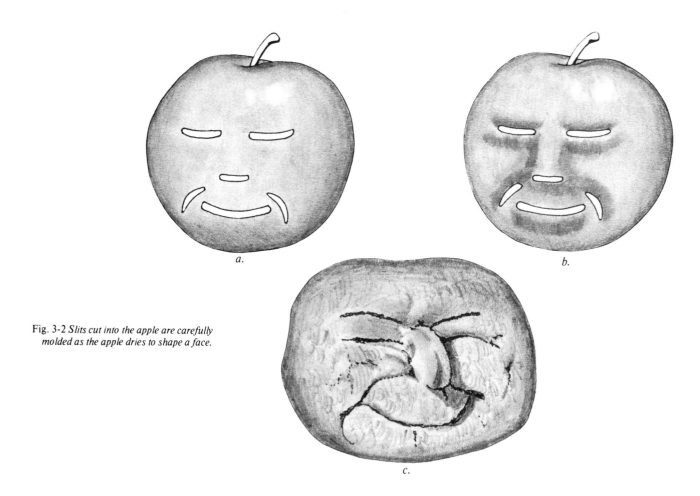

a.

b.

c.

Fig. 3-2 *Slits cut into the apple are carefully molded as the apple dries to shape a face.*

along the edges of the nose. Others actually carve the features from the apple (Fig. 3-5), but I prefer to mold these in as the apple dries.

If you do try carving the features, be sure to space them widely, as the apple shrinks to about half its original size when dry. Soak the apple for an hour in pure lemon juice (a container of which may be frozen for reuse with subsequent dolls).

Put a long piece of wire through the core and make loops at either end. Hang the apple in an airy spot out of the sun, and let it dry two or three days. If you have carved the features, you may be able to just let it dry of its own accord; if you have just made slits, as I do, it is time to begin forming the face.

Use the eraser end of a pencil and begin pushing carefully to form features. Push in for the eyes and around the nose. Do this gently; you have several weeks to work on each head, and it is better to do a little each day until the features begin to take shape (Fig. 3-2b).

You may find that you have to make a tiny cut above the mouth for the bottom of the nose. Push the eye sockets toward the center to form a ridge for the bridge of the nose, pinch the cheeks to form the hollows beside the nose. Push upward from the eye socket and down from the forehead to form brows.

By working slowly you can form more character in the face and have more natural-looking features. After about a month, the apple should be dry (Fig. 3-2c).

If the doll is to have apple hands, make these when you begin the head. Cut several slices of apple, soak in lemon juice, and hang them on thread to dry. When they have dried enough to be cut with scissors, make snips for the four fingers and cut a wedge out to form the thumb (Fig. 3-3). I make several hands so I'll have a better chance of getting a good pair. As they dry, form the fingers by pinching and separating them.

When hands and head are thoroughly dry, it is time to begin the body. I don't even decide what the character will be until the head is dry, because heads will suggest different dolls. One will look like a weary old farmer, others are definitely old ladies' faces.

By making several heads at a time, you will have a good selection to choose from. Some you may not like at all, so it is best to have some leeway.

Pull the wire so that the top loop is against the head. Bend the loop down flat so it can be covered with hair. A drop of white glue at the loop end will help hold the head in place. Make a small bend in the wire below the head, or a tiny loop, just to hold the head in place. This will be covered later.

Cut another wire the length of both arms and twist it around the body wire. Now loop the body wire around it so neither can slip. Keeping the body in proportion with the head, bend the wire at the hip and again at the foot, doubling wire back to the hip and down again to form the other leg (Fig. 3-4a,b).

Another method is to use a double wire all along, pushing both ends through the head and hanging the drying apple from the resulting loop. In this way the arms can be formed from the main wire (Fig. 3-4c). It makes a stronger doll, but apple-head dolls are decorative pieces, not subject to much strain, so this is not very important.

Originally, many apple-head dolls were done with cornhusk bodies made from large field cornhusks, but since we plan to dress the doll,

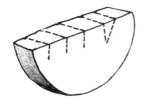

Fig. 3-3 *A slice of apple makes a hand.*

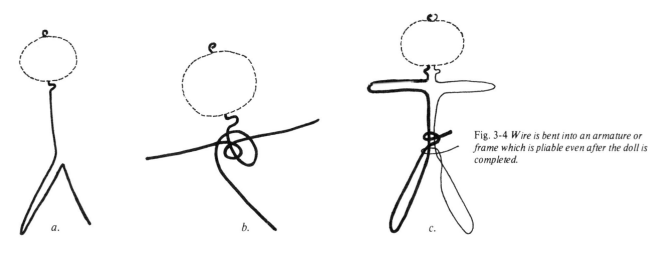

Fig. 3-4 *Wire is bent into an armature or frame which is pliable even after the doll is completed.*

a.

b.

c.

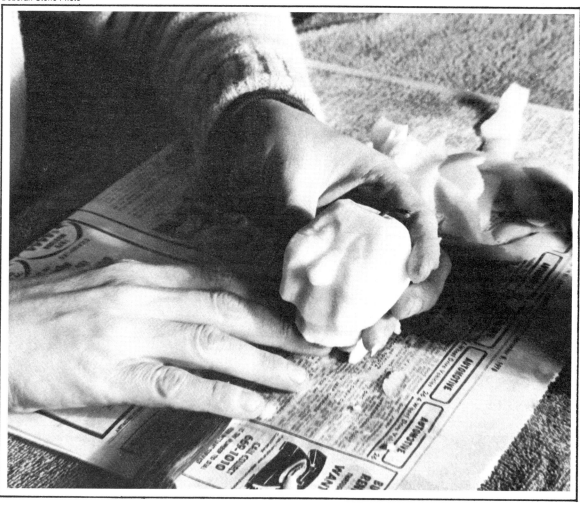

Fig. 3-5 Some doll makers prefer to actually carve a rough face into the freshly peeled apple.

wrapped wire is more suitable. The wire may be wrapped with any number of materials. Wool fleece covered with strips of nylon stocking makes a skin-colored wrapping, but since none of the wrapped part shows on the finished doll, nearly any fabric can be used. Extra padding or wrapping fills out the body.

Once the form is made and wrapped, arms and legs can be bent to any position. If the single wire was used, hands may be attached by sticking the wire into the wrists. If the double-wire method was used, make a small slit in the wrist to push the loop into. In either case, secure with a drop of white glue.

Dressing the doll can be at your own whim or fancy. Use solids or miniature calico and gingham prints. Well-worn denim will be soft enough for overalls. Wide lace can be a shawl or a dressy apron for a grannie. Tiny leftover pieces of trims can be glued or stitched to the wrists for cuffs.

Felt or worn-out kid gloves can be made into shoes or boots. Raw wool makes perfect hair, since its color and texture are appropriate for

Apple-Head Dolls

the wrinkled skin of the face. It can be wrapped around, braided or just glued on in disarray. Strips of it can be glued in place for bushy eyebrows or mustaches and beards.

The face can be accented by using tiny beads tucked into the eyes, a faint touch of pink on the cheeks and a dot of red on the mouth.

Clothing and accessories can be made in many ways. A fisherman would have a little knit cap, a woodsman an axe made of wood, a housewife or a witch a broom made of cornhusks or grass tied to a small stick.

Sweaters can be made from worn-out stockings, eyeglasses from fine wire, jewelry from Indian beads. Little bouquets of dried flowers or herbs can be carried in bundles or baskets. The baskets can be woven from cornhusks or iris leaves (dried and then dampened for weaving). If you can knit, try knitting a tiny piece with fine yarn on very fine needles, then transfer it to two round toothpicks for the doll to hold.

The only problem with apple-head dolls is that they have so much personality in their old faces, I find myself talking to them! ✱

Fig. 3-6 *After drying, many faces will suggest the character of the doll they will become. This one suggested a witch to doll maker Allyn Lurgio.*

CHAPTER 4

Braiding a Rug

Rug braiding is a craft younger than the era of decoration we usually associate it with. Because of its visual affinity to the simple lines of early Colonial furniture, we think of it in that era, but historical evidence points to its origin in the late 1820s and its rise to popularity in the 1830s. Handloomed woolens were too precious for such use: thus the luxury of thick braided rugs had to wait for the advent of mechanical weaving.

Although such things are hard to pinpoint, rug braiding appears to have begun in New England. It is easy to see why. The cold winters made heavy floor coverings necessary, and the native sense of thrift made such a use of old clothing attractive.

Most braided rugs, except those done professionally, are still made from old clothing, with occasional purchased wool added for special color or when supplies run out. While the fancy fabrics and the cotton scraps go into the quilt basket, woolens still go in the rug bag.

The variety of usable woolens is almost endless. Everything, from the finest of doeskin flannel to heavy blanket fabric, is braidable; the two extremes can often even be combined in the same rug if the strips are in different widths.

The first step, then, is collecting the wool. A thorough closet and attic cleaning will usually turn up a fair start. Be sure the fabrics are wool, not synthetics, since the latter do not wear as well or as evenly. If you sew, your sewing scraps may also contain large enough pieces.

From your attic, progress to your friends' attics. Let it be known

Fig. 4-1 *No floor covering brings more warmth to a country setting than a hand-braided rug.*

that you are braiding a rug and need any discarded woolen clothes. Even badly worn clothing will have usable areas of fabric. Rummage sales, yard sales and thrift shops will often provide ample supplies at very low prices.

When all else fails, or if you want different colors, you can buy rug wool by the pound very reasonably. If you don't find the colors you want, buy light shades or white and dye them yourself to suit. Remnant tables are often a good source of fabric more expensive than bulk, but cheaper than bolt wool.

Before you purchase wool, it is a good idea to sort out what you have and prepare it for braiding. Cut garments apart at the seams, remove (and save!) buttons, zippers, etc. Wash all these flat pieces in mild soap, rinse well and dry. This shrinks the fabric and fluffs it, and is a very important step.

Cut or tear the fabric into strips, always on the straight of the fabric, not a bias. There is a great discussion among braiders over the best size for the braid. This is, of course, determined by the width of the strips and must be decided upon before the fabric is cut.

Narrow braid is generally considered to be more professional and is preferred by many experienced braiders as a finer form of the craft. I think it depends upon the use for the rug: the more informal the setting, the wider the braid. I like fat braid because the colors tend to show up better and the rug is thicker. But be careful not to place the finished fat-braid rug in the way of doors which might not clear its thickness.

My suggestion is that you cut three sample strips of medium-weight wool about two inches wide and braid them together for about five inches to see if you like the size. If you do, use that as your base width. If you are doubtful, cut three more 1½ inches wide and braid these for comparison. When you have decided which size braid you prefer, keep the sample braid. Cut all medium-weight woolens to that width; cut thicker fabrics narrower and finer fabrics wider. (To know exactly how wide to cut strips of a particular fabric, cut a test strip and try braiding it into your sample braid. If the braid remains even, you are cutting the fabric the right width. After a while, you will be able to judge by just rolling the fabric between your fingers.) If you can rip the woolens, do so, since it is both easier and faster, and you get a straighter strip. Some you will have to cut. As each color is cut in strips, roll it into flat rolls and secure with rubber bands.

When all the fabric is prepared, sort it out by color. Separate solids, tweeds and plaids within each color range. From this you can begin to plan your rug. If you need other colors for accent or to match a room, you can easily tell at this point.

It is difficult to know exactly how much wool you will need of each color, especially since your recycled wool doesn't come by the yard. In figuring yardage on new fabric, figure about a yard of material 54-60 inches wide for each square foot. That's easy to calculate: just multiply the width of the rug by the length, and the answer will be the yardage. A rug four by six feet takes 24 yards. To translate this to pounds (it is easier to weigh rolls of recycled fabric), figure about two-thirds of a pound of medium-weight woolens per square foot of rug.

If you are buying by the pound, remember that there will be wasted edges when you cut and allow for that. Therefore, when buying bulk fabric, figure three-quarters of a pound to give you a square foot of rug.

In planning how to combine colors, think of the room the rug will be in. If you wish to have a color predominate, plan to use several rows of it together in solid band about halfway through the rug. You can blend it in by using one strand of it with two others for one round, two strands for the next round, then several rows of solid color. Blend it out on the outer edge by introducing one strand of the next color for one row, then another with only one strand of your main color. It is a good idea to do this whenever you move to a new color (Fig. 4-8).

Your rug can have stripes of different colors or can be entirely a tweed effect. My favorite rugs combine solid bands with areas of tweed. You can make a general plan for your rug on paper first, using crayons to give you an idea of the visual effect of the colors and pattern and how the various colors will blend.

Since recycled woolens tend to be heavy on grays, browns and drab colors, you can use these as your third strands and as fillers for background areas. Use one or two strands of these neutral colors to stretch out fabric you don't have a lot of, or to tone down very bright colors.

You can join your strips into longer ones ahead of time if you have a lot of short pieces, but it is easier to braid with fairly short strips and add as you go. To join pieces, place them together at right angles and stitch firmly on the bias. Trim the edges. Be sure the raw seam edges all face the inside (Fig. 4-2).

The actual braiding process is quite easy. The raw edges must be folded in as you braid, and, for a reversible rug, you should keep the seams (the open edges) on the right side all the time. This open edge will be joined to the rug and will thus be covered as you lace the rug together.

You can use little metal clips called Braid-Aids to fold in the raw edges, but I find it just as easy to fold the strips as I braid. Very soon this becomes almost automatic, and the raw edges roll themselves into place in the center when you pull on the strips. I do find it is easier for children to work with the Braid-Aids since their hands are too small to do both things at once.

To begin the braid, stitch together two of the first three strands on the bias into a straight strip. Fold it lengthwise and stitch the end of the third strand into the center of the fold, forming a "T" (Fig. 4-3). Don't put it directly on the first seam. Trim the three strips to different lengths if they are the same. (At any subsequent point in the braiding if you notice two strips the same length, cut one off so your joining seams aren't in the same place.)

If you have a braiding clamp, fasten the end into the clamp. I find a

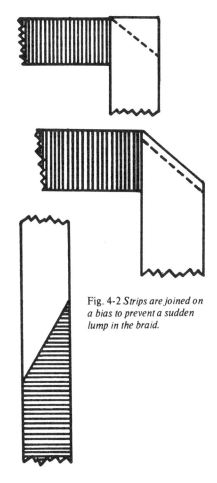

Fig. 4-2 *Strips are joined on a bias to prevent a sudden lump in the braid.*

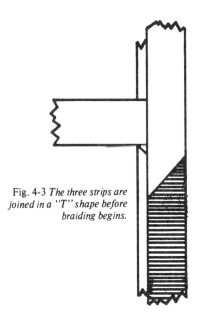

Fig. 4-3 *The three strips are joined in a "T" shape before braiding begins.*

Fig. 4-4 *The braid should be neat, even and tight.*

clipboard works well, and as the braid lengthens I can hold it down with my foot. My daughter closes the end of her braid in the drawer on the kitchen table. Use any system that works for you and allows you to move the braid away from you as you work.

As you braid, keep the strands straight without twisting them. Hold the "tails" out at right angles to the braid, not down straight. This will give you a tighter, rounder braid (Fig. 4-4). If you are in doubt about whether your braid is tight enough, try to poke a pencil (eraser end) through it. If you can, you need to tighten the braid.

Be sure your braid is even, tight and round. If it isn't, undo it back to the problem point and re-do it. As you need to, add more strips, sewing them on the bias and working the seam into a hidden position in the braid.

Before you begin to braid you must decide, if not the exact size, at least the proportion of the finished rug so you will know what size to make the center braid. This length determines the difference between the length and width of the rug, hence a rug three by five feet or four by six feet would have a two-foot braid. Simply subtract the width from the length.

This center braid is first made twice the length determined, then folded back against itself and laced together into one double length. The rest of the rug is laced on to this center in a continuing clockwise spiral (counter-clockwise if you are left-handed).

One of the most difficult parts of the rug is making that first sharp bend at the end of the first row lie flat. But there is a simple trick to make it lie perfectly. Complete the center braid to the proper length, ending it with the left-hand strand on the bottom, the middle strand on top and facing left, and the right-hand strand also on the bottom.

Twist the left and center strands over one another without braiding in the right strand as follows: left over center and left over center again. Then braid in the right-hand strand tightly, and you will see your braid begin to curl right around smoothly and completely flat. Do this once more and you have made the corner and have your colors back in the right sequence again (Fig. 4-5).

When you have braided your double center braid and enough for about another round, you are ready to begin lacing it together. It is best to lace as you go along or you won't know when to change colors.

Lacing is done from the reverse side and clockwise. If you go counter-clockwise, you will always be working across the entire width

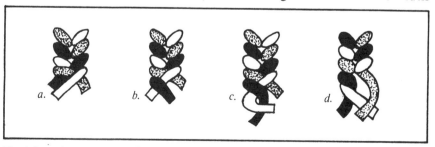

a.   b.   c.   d.

Fig. 4-5 *The first corner will lie flat if one strand is skipped in the braiding at the end of the center braid.*

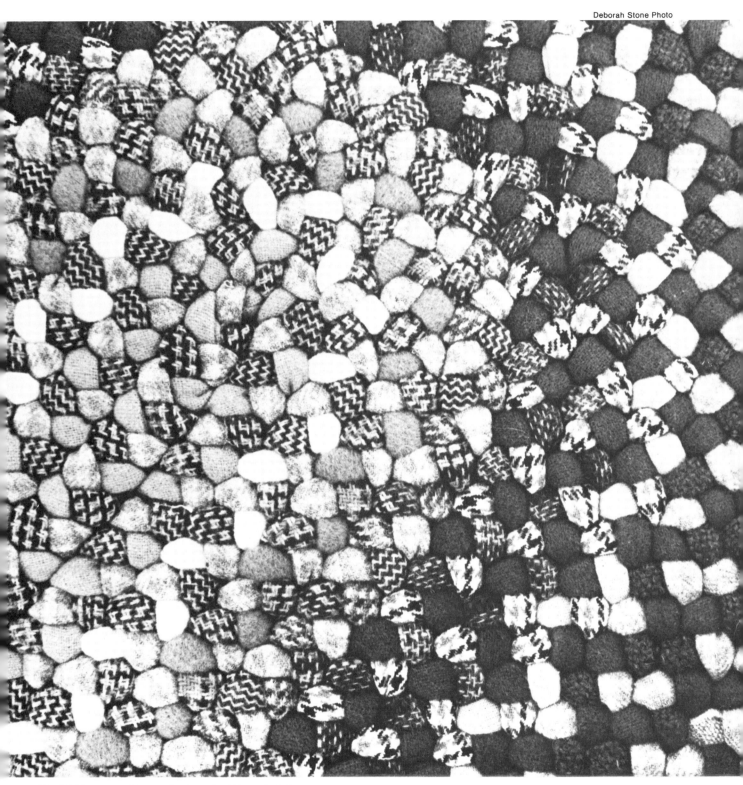

Fig. 4-6 *The center of the completed rug should be perfectly flat.*

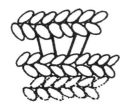

Fig. 4-7 *As the rug becomes larger with each successive round, the lacing must accommodate this increase by skipping a loop on the braid as it is attached to the body of the rug.*

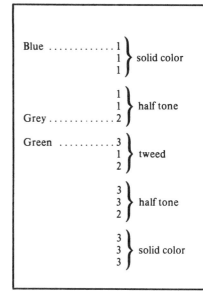

Blue ....1 ⎫
         1 ⎬ solid color
         1 ⎭

         1 ⎫
         1 ⎬ half tone
Grey ....2 ⎭

Green ....3 ⎫
         1 ⎬ tweed
         2 ⎭

         3 ⎫
         3 ⎬ half tone
         2 ⎭

         3 ⎫
         3 ⎬ solid color
         3 ⎭

Fig. 4-8 *To switch from a solid blue at the center of your rug to a green stripe, the above procedure is recommended. Starting with three strands of blue in the center braids, introduce one strand of a grey or neutral shade for a half tone, then move to a tweed effect by braiding one strand of blue, one grey, and one of green. Progress to a green half tone by substituting a second green strand for the blue, and then ease into three strands of green to produce your stripe. Always introduce new color into the right-hand tube.*

of the rug, a most awkward position (unless, of course, you are left-handed). Lacing is always done on a flat surface.

The first two rows have to be sewn together to form the center braid; from there on you should lace the braids together using a blunt-ended lacing needle. There is a special carpet thread made for this purpose.

The braid should be placed so the loops fit into one another — that is, the loops on one braid should fit into the dents on the next. Bring the lacing needle under the loop on the inside (toward the side being joined) and up through the braid. Don't put it through the fabric. Keep going under a loop and up through the braid, moving from one braid to the other and pulling the thread tightly. The rug will be tight and flat.

When you get to the curves (there are four) you have to skip a loop every so often on the braid (not on the rug) to make up for the increase in the size of each round (Fig. 4-7). If you don't accommodate this extra length of each row, you will have a beautiful braided bowl instead of a rug! Do this on the four curves, but not in exactly the same spot each time. As you lace, you will be able to tell when it's time to skip a loop because the braid will begin to pull your lacing at an angle.

These curves are also where you change colors, and to keep your rug symmetrical, you should always change on the same curve, in a line. As mentioned before, change only one strand of color at a time to blend the colors smoothly (Fig. 4-8).

Your rug will begin to take shape very quickly and the first few feet in diameter will go very fast. As it begins to look like a rug, you will gain confidence in your braiding. You have learned in the first several rounds just about all you need to know to braid a beautiful rug.

When it is the size you want, braid it to the curve where you have changed colors. Cut the strips at different lengths about two inches apart and taper them back about five inches for narrow braid, eight inches for wide braid. Continue to braid until you can't tuck the edges in, then blind-stitch the edges under and braid, tapering down to a final strip which covers the ends of the other two. Tuck in any raw edges and blind-stitch this final strip in place (Fig. 4-9).

Your rug is now completed, and you will want to care for it as the precious heirloom it is. Never hang it or use a carpet beater on it. I know your grandmother did, but it will weaken your rug and shorten its life. She never thought of her braided rug as a piece of art for all ages' you know better.

Vacuum it as you would any rug; treat stains immediately. When your rug needs cleaning, use a powdered cleaner that you brush in, then vacuum out. If you store or move your rug, roll it. Never fold a braided rug.

If your rug does meet with sudden disaster, work quickly and remember that such rugs have withstood generations of children no messier than yours. Julie once overturned an entire jar of kelly green tempera paint on one of ours. We scrubbed it immediately with water and mild soap and when we were finished, we were astonished to find that instead of a dirty spot, we had a clean spot! We'd forgotten how bright the colors had been when the rug was new! ✴

Fig. 4-9 *The rug is completed by narrowing the strips and the resulting braid until it can be stitched inconspicuously into the edge of the rug.*

CHAPTER

5

Bronze Stenciling

The decorative techniques of bronze stenciling, while of common origin, seem to have had two very separate purposes in the American Colonies and into later years.

Fashionable ladies with time to spare were following their English counterparts in learning the art of decorating trays in bronze. Meanwhile in more meagre homes, furniture was often made of scrap wood of different kinds, not all of which matched or was attractive. To cover these discrepancies, furniture was often painted and some form of decoration applied to dress it up. A natural direction for this ornamentation to take was toward the elegant oriental lacquered pieces that graced more pretentious homes.

The technique for decorating a tray or a chair is exactly the same once the surface is prepared, and even there, the two mediums are similar.

While our ancestors were working with new wood or tin, we are often restoring their work and must begin by making the surface as nearly like the original as possible. New tin and wooden articles suitable for decoration are available, and if you use these, skip lightly over this next series of directions.

Before you begin to remove anything except accumulated dirt, check the piece *carefully* for remnants of old decoration. Even the smallest or least attractive design is worth recording, even if you choose to use another when you restore the piece. Many designs used by early craftsmen were original, or at least not mass produced, and

Fig. 5-1 *A plain kitchen chair is a good stenciling project, as most were originally painted.*

Fig. 5-2 *This box, decorated by Jan Krise of Richmond, New Hampshire, is a reproduction of a box by Ransom Cook, a famous early 19th-century New York stenciler. The pattern dates from between 1823 and 1834.*

Fig. 5-3 *A small wooden box is a perfect item for stenciled decoration. This design is by Jan Krise, who has stenciled for Old Sturbridge Village.*

the pattern you have may be the only one left of its kind.

To record a design, clean the surface carefully to expose as much of the old pattern as possible, then outline the design with a silver-leaded pencil. (These pencils are available at art supply stores and are very inexpensive.) If you can't get a silver-leaded pencil, use a white-leaded pencil. Since designs were usually stenciled on black or dark-color backgrounds, this tracing will make them show up. If the background color is light, you may not have to do this.

In a good light, trace the design on to thin tracing paper. If the outline is too obscure to show up through the tracing paper, trace it directly on to clear plastic wrap, using all-surface, fine-pointed marking pens. When dry, the plastic wrap is then laid on white paper for contrast; now cover the traced design with tracing paper and transfer the design to that. Make notes as to colors and other important details.

Now that you have done your duty for posterity, you are free to strip away paint in good conscience. It is possible, however, that in this careful cleaning process, you may discover that the decoration is complete enough, and the old surface repairable enough that you want to save it in its present form, and learn stenciling on something else. I am almost incapable of refinishing anything with any old decoration on it!

But assuming there is nothing worth keeping, use any of the commercial paint removers on the market. Read the directions before buying to be sure you have one you can use easily. Some need to be hosed off with water, which is difficult in a city apartment! Use an old toothbrush to get all old paint out of ridges, corners, etc. If the piece is tin, wash it well in detergent and water, then in clean water after the old finish is removed. Use a rusticide and/or steel wool to remove any rust, and wash again and rinse well. Dry all surfaces thoroughly so new rust won't form, and leave the piece to dry completely for a few hours. New tin need only be washed and rinsed well.

Apply a coat of primer paint (use one made for metal) thinned to the consistency of milk. If brush marks show, it needs more thinning. Dry 24 hours and rub very softly with the finest wet-dry sandpaper dipped in water. Dry and repeat with a second coat only if needed.

Apply a coat of flat black enamel, also thinned to milk consistency, using a soft brush. Let dry 24 hours and sand as before. Remove every trace of sanding and other lint, using an old nylon stocking or a linen towel. Repeat with a second and, if necessary, a third coat of enamel until the surface is evenly covered and smooth.

If your piece is wood, whether new or stripped, first sand perfectly smooth with sandpaper. If the wood has a very coarse grain, fill it with any commercial wood filler and sand smooth. Apply a thin coat of shellac and sand with fine finishing paper. Wipe clean with a rag dampened in turpentine. Apply flat enamel and sand as for tin.

The next step for tin or wood is varnishing. This is done in as dust-free and environment as possible to keep the finish perfectly smooth. Use a new can of varnish and a one-inch varnish brush. I pour a new can into several small (baby-food) jars and seal each very tightly. A partly full jar or can will thicken with exposure to air inside the can and will not be suitable for use in bronze stenciling.

Varnishing is best done on a dry day, with the varnish and the surface both at room temperature. Be sure surface is free of dust. Pour a little varnish into a clean container, and wet the brush in it. Wipe this first brushful off on an old magazine. Dip your brush again and let the excess drip off (don't wipe on the edge of the container). Working quickly and in one direction, flow varnish onto the surface in an even coat. Don't go back over any section except to catch a bare spot — and do that immediately.

If you are doing a tray or a small item, put it in a box with the lid propped slightly open. This protects it from dust but still allows air flow. Be sure it is level so the varnish won't run. Dry 48 hours.

All this drudgery is necessary if your finished piece is to look right. It is a waste of time to put a design on a poorly prepared surface, for it will neither look right nor last.

Trace the stencil pattern on the dull side of the architect's linen. If it is all flat work without overlays, use one piece of stencil paper for the

Fig. 5-4 *This pattern was reproduced from the remnants of one found on a thumb-back chair from the Wyman Tavern in Keene, New Hampshire.*

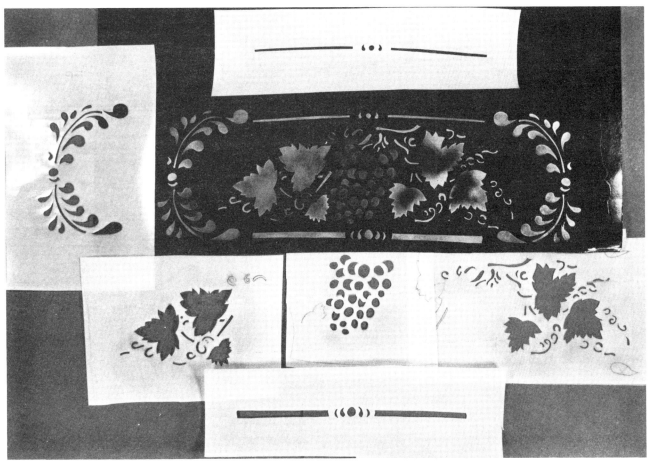

Deborah Stone Photo

Fig. 5-5 *A palette of bronze powders on a piece of cotton velvet.*

Deborah Stone Photo

whole pattern, even though the colors change. If, however, one part of the design touches or laps over another, use separate pieces.

Cut the stencil with an X-Acto knife (use a new blade) and very small scissors. You can purchase special scissors for this or substitute a good pair of manicure scissors. Don't cut to the tip of the blades; hold the stencil in place and reopen the blades instead. Move the paper, not the cutting edge, in cutting curves.

If any one shape (grapes, leaves, etc.) is used many times, cut only one stencil of it and move it around. Be sure all edges are clean cut. A fuzzy edge will ruin your work. If you cut on a piece of glass, knife cuts will be smoother.

At this point, I always test out a stencil on a piece of cardboard painted with flat black enamel (you can buy special black-surfaced cardboard for this). It is not essential, but it gives you a chance to make any changes, find errors, and see the finished design before doing it on the finished piece. Also, it gives you a permanent record of the pattern, which is handy (Fig. 5-4).

To do this, follow the directions below for the stenciling of the tin or wood piece, but use the black cardboard.

Varnish the entire surface to be stenciled, using slightly thinned varnish. Let dry at least 2 hours and press a corner of the stencil, shiny side down, onto the varnish. Pull it off. If it snaps off, the varnish is at the right stage of tackiness; if not, continue testing every 15 minutes until it snaps.

Prepare a velveteen palette from a piece of dark velveteen (eight or ten inches wide by ten or twelve inches long) whose edges are bound with masking tape. Choose the colors of bronze powder you will use,

Bronze Stenciling

and tap a very *little* powder from each vial onto the palette (Fig. 5-5). Make "bobs" from pieces of velveteen which you wrap around your finger to transfer the powder from the palette to the stencil. You will need a different bob for each color used, and it is best to cover the edges of these with masking tape, too.

When the varnish has reached the right tackiness, place the stencil, shiny side down, where you want the design to appear. Press the stencil down firmly.

Pick up a bit of bronze powder from the palette with a bob. Rub off any excess from the bob on another scrap of velveteen. Push down the bronzed bob all over the area to be colored. Polish the area with the bob, using a circular motion, working from the cut edges of the stencil opening towards the center. If the object is round, a rounded effect is created by making the color stronger on the edges, and lighter towards the center. Or you can highlight a center by making *it* more strongly colored and letting the color fade to the edges.

Flowers should be bronzed more heavily in the center and lightly on the edges. Make leaves heavy on the tips and edges, leaving the center and base very lightly bronzed. Do veins and stems with a separate stencil, always remembering to change bobs when you change colors.

When the design is completed, let the varnish dry for 24 hours. Clean the stencils well with rags moistened in turpentine.

If, when the work is dry, you are not happy with it, or you see an error, scrub that portion with a damp rag dipped in powdered cleanser (Ajax, Comet, etc.) to remove the bronze, and redo it. You will, of course, need another coat of "tacky" varnish.

Leaf veins, tendrils, or other lines for highlighting can be added with a brush after the tacky varnish has dried 24 hours. Work a drop of varnish into a little bronze powder (on a plate, not the velveteen palette) until it makes a bronze paint. Then, using a fine-pointed sable brush (size 0), paint in stems, veins, tendrils and other lines freehand.

Pat the finished stenciled area with a damp cloth and wash it by rubbing it with your soapy hand, using a lot of water to remove any excess bronze powder. Rinse, wipe dry, and varnish with two coats to seal. Dry and sand lightly with very fine wetted sandpaper between coats.

When the piece is finished and varnished, you can add such touches as striping (p. 84). This was done on most stenciled pieces, both to highlight turnings in rungs and to outline or frame flat areas and chair seats, giving the chair or tray a more finished look.

Many different items were originally decorated with stenciling. Bureaux, chairs, and small tables were the most commonly done furniture, while any tin that wasn't a tool might have been decorated. Boxes, trays, bowls (not milk pans), sconces, and flat pieces were most commonly done. I even have an old stenciled slops pail of great artistic charm, though such mundane items were not usually so graced! ✸

CHAPTER

6

Theorem Painting

Theorem painting, or stenciling on white velvet, is a 19th-century art. It was popular not only for the beauty of the finished work, but because this result could be accomplished by anyone who worked carefully. Artistic talent is not essential to good theorem painting.

The soft delicate shades of theorem painting are distinctive, but not difficult to achieve. The most tedious part of the process is cutting the stencils.

Good patterns for theorem painting are those taken from old stenciled objects and can be found in books on bronze stenciling. Once you have gained a little experience, you will want to make your own patterns, but the old patterns will give you a good start. One favorite subject was a basket of fruit, a pattern with a variety of colors and a minimum of freehand work.

Stencils are cut on architect's linen using an X-Acto knife and manicure scissors. There are special scissors made for stencil cutting, but good manicure scissors will do for the beginner. A piece of window glass with the edges taped for safety is a good surface to cut against.

The more carefully you cut your stencils, the better your work will be. Rough edges make fuzzy lines. Be sure your blade is *sharp*. For your first attempt, try the project design reproduced here. Draw or trace the outlines of the design. Think of each outlined area as a hole in your stencils. Starting at the center, number as many separate areas

Fig. 6-1 *An antique frame highlights the theorem painting of an old bowl-of-fruit pattern done by Mary Ann Williams of Keene, New Hampshire.*

as do not touch each other as No. 1. Beginning at the center again, number a new series of separate, non-touching parts 2. No. 2 areas may touch No. 1 areas, but NOT EACH OTHER. Continue as needed with No. 3, and subsequent numbered areas if needed. Usually three or four numbers are quite enough. Remember that each numbered area may touch areas carrying another number, but not those bearing its own number (Fig. 6-2).

Unlike other forms of stenciling, theorem does not require a separate stencil for each color. As long as the areas are not contiguous, they can be rendered in different colors from the same stencil. If there is a space between elements in the design, they may carry the same number.

All the areas numbered "1" will be cut into your Number One stencil, all the areas numbered "2", into the Number Two stencil, and so on. Therefore, as the numbered diagram shows, for this design you will have to cut three stencils.

This numbered design is your master theorem from which all the stencils will be cut. Draw a rectangular border around the design, framing it by about one inch. This will serve as a guide for registering your successive stencils so that all the areas will be painted in the right places on the velvet (Fig. 6-3).

Cut a template of cardboard to the measure of this border frame. This will eliminate tedious measuring and squaring off border-frame guidelines on each stencil. Once you have the template, simply center on the design and draw around it — on the stencils and on the paper or velvet.

On a piece of linen-finish art paper (Strathmore is the most like velvet), draw the border of your theorem. Tape the stencils 1,2, and 3

Fig. 6-2 *Each element of the pattern is numbered so that no touching parts are cut on the same stencil.*

Theorem Painting

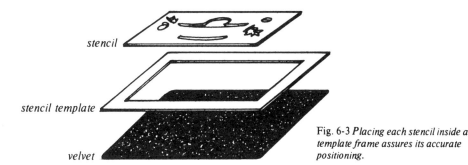

stencil

stencil template

velvet

Fig. 6-3 *Placing each stencil inside a template frame assures its accurate positioning.*

etc. down, one at a time, to the paper, matching borders, and paint the design on the paper.

For paint you will need small tubes (since very little is used) of transparent oil paint in the basic colors: cadmium red medium, chrome yellow, prussian blue, burnt umber, and vert emeraud. Put a little dab of each on your palette or a piece of foil.

Cut a piece of wool flannel about four inches square for each color you will use. Put this over your finger and barely touch it in the paint. Rub it on a scrap of cloth until most of the paint is off. Working from the edge to the center of each cut-out area in the stencil, paint with soft, light strokes, repeating with the other stencils, being careful to keep each successive stencil in correct register, until the entire picture appears painted on the art paper.

If you are doing a design with a lot of foliage, mix several shades of green on the palette, some more blue, some more yellow, some with a speck of umber. This will give variety and depth to the finished work.

Leave a small area uncolored in each shape, especially in rounded objects like fruit, to form highlights. This highlighting is characteristic of theorem and it is important to achieve roundness and dimension (Fig. 6-4).

If you need to inspect the work as you go, always leave one side taped firmly so you can replace the stencil accurately. When completed, this sample will be your guide as you do the velvet, and it will serve as a permanent record to keep with the stencils.

From this sample you will be able to improve your final work. Don't expect it to look like a finished painting, since it is on paper, not velvet. When you are satisfied that your stencil and colors are right, you are ready to begin the real thing.

You will need an off-white or cream-colored cotton velvet (often called velveteen). If you are unable to get this color, use plain white and dip it in a solution of hot tea. Lay the fabric out flat to dry. In storing your velvet, roll it rather than fold it to prevent damage to the nap. Once it is rolled, store the velvet on its side, not on its end.

Cut a piece of heavy cardboard the size of your finished project and paint it with white glue. Smooth it so there are no puddles ... it

Fig. 6-4 *Rounded shapes are given dimension by a highlight.*

should just be tacky. Lay the dry velvet on the board face-up and smooth out all wrinkles, lifting and pulling the edges slightly to get a perfect surface.

For a mount larger than five by seven inches, it helps to apply glue in two-inch strips and roll the velvet on to one strip at a time. Keep the remaining velvet folded back over the part you've already glued.

Velvet has a tendency to leave little spots of nap wherever it goes. Be sure none of this lint (or any raveling) gets on the back of the velvet or the glued surface of the cardboard mount.

When the glue has dried, center your first stencil on the fabric and secure both to your work surface with masking tape. Using the paper pattern as a guide, start from the outside edge of each stencil opening and brush lightly toward the center. Continue all around the edge, leaving a small highlight in the middle as you did on the paper. Always work lightly, repeating in areas where darker color is required. Work *with* the nap of the velvet.

If you have trouble with smudges outside the stencil area, cut a mask of white paper to cover the velvet and the edges of the stencils.

Theorem Painting Directions

for the fruit basket design

Paint the pear yellow, darker at the edges, lighter towards the center. Paint the larger section of the peach yellow, blushing to orange from the center right up to the crease. The color line separates the sections, as the small section on the right is all yellow.

The melon is painted yellow first; then paint over the yellow with green at the edges, leaving the centers yellow. Paint all the grapes purple, darker at the edges, and highlight the center of each. Paint the cherries red; then paint over the edges with darker red (use black to darken the first red), leaving the centers bright red.

The strawberries are yellow, shaded with red, having the edges and the tops darker, the center and bottoms lighter. Paint the basket yellow, then shade one side of each strip with yellow mixed with umber.

Paint the stems and tendrils brown, and the leaves green. Leaves should be darker at the edges, lighter in the center.

Make any necessary corrections freehand with a fine brush. Paint darker veins on the leaves, and touch up any places where the colors didn't meet. Paint yellow seeds on the strawberries freehand.

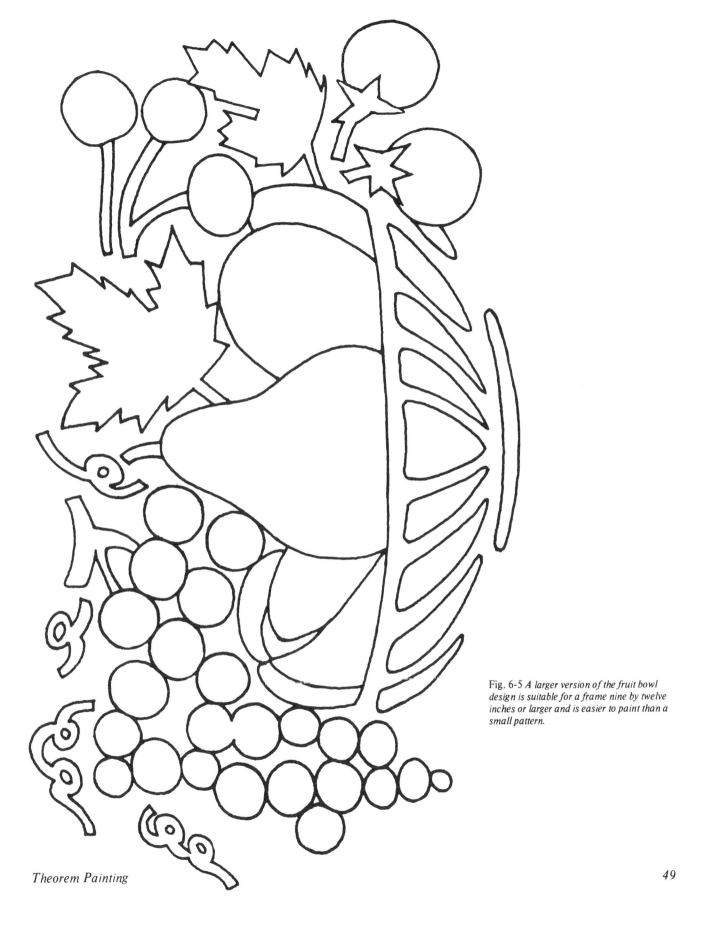

Fig. 6-5 *A larger version of the fruit bowl design is suitable for a frame nine by twelve inches or larger and is easier to paint than a small pattern.*

Fig. 6-6 *This beautiful and complex theorem was done by a 19th-century expert. (Courtesy Museum of the Concord Antiquarian Society, Concord, Massachusetts.)*

Fig. 6-7 *Simple fruit arrangements lend themselves to theorem. These are both by Judith Lund of South Dartmouth, Massachusetts.*

Theorem Painting

Fig. 6-8 *Designs such as these can be traced from old flower prints.*

Wipe all pencil marks off your stencils before using them.

Although the stencils are the same, the result will be slightly different each time you use them. Sometimes there will be a little white space between the shapes. When this happens, replace the stencil and edge it up to the next area to cover the white space and paint just that edge very carefully.

If you happen to make a little spot on the velvet where you didn't mean to, you can't remove it, but often you can cover it with a small stenciled design added for that purpose: a spot beside a bouquet of flowers could be covered with an extra leaf, a bee or even a butterfly. A few grapes or berries could be added to a fruit bowl.

When you are finished, clean the stencils with turpentine (never get water on them), and dry them well before storing.

Now you are ready for the freehand touches that will make the theorem distinctively yours, even if you copied the design from a book.

With a sable artist's brush #00 or #1 add stems, leaf veins and other touches with burnt umber thinned with rectified turpentine. Test it on a paint rag to be sure it won't run.

As you become more experienced, you will want to experiment with special effects and more complicated patterns. You can overlap design areas, or add a shading of one color on top of another (to give the blush to a peach, for example).

The theorem form of art is especially suited to flowers and fruit and as you work with it, you will find yourself eyeing pictures with the thought of making them into stencils. Old flower prints are a good source of patterns. Try making your own numbered theorem patterns for pictures. Two other designs to try are shown in Fig. 6-8.　✹

CHAPTER 7

Patchwork and Quilting

Of all the beautiful handwork done throughout our history, none captures the spirit of our heritage quite like the patchwork quilt. The very idea of making warm, useful and beautiful objects from fabric scraps too small for other use is the essence of the spirit that kept the Colonies, and later the new nation, alive.

But beyond sheer survival, the way in which these tiny pieces of different fabrics were combined gave outlet and are testimony to the finest artistic instincts of women whose sparse lives held little time for beauty. It was an occupation that spanned ages; small girls and their grandmothers stitched side by side. A lonely frontier wife could make a quilt, as could a group of ladies in town.

There are two distinct needlework skills in making a pieced quilt: the patchwork and the quilting. The first consists of cutting all the little pieces to the right sizes and shapes and stitching them together to form blocks. The blocks are then assembled to make a quilt top. The top is put together with the backing and a layer of batting in between.

The second skill is the quilting itself, which is done by making row upon row of tiny running stitches through all three layers to hold the batting in place. As with the designs of the blocks themselves, the quilting may be simple or very intricate.

It is possible to enjoy the craft of patchwork without doing quilting. Coverlets or bedspreads may be made from the finished quilt top, or single squares (blocks) may be made into pillows or chair mats (the latter may even be quilted).

Fig. 7-1 *This modern quilt was worked in a ubiquitous pattern known by many different names, including Goose Foot and Turkey Trot. By Deborah Stone of Peterborough, New Hampshire.*

Patchwork and Quilting

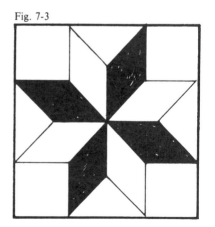

Fig. 7-2 *The pattern can be split into smaller pieces for a more intricate effect.*

To begin a quilt, or a single block, it is a good idea to assemble all the fabric and take stock.

The best material is cotton or cotton-dacron blend about the weight of a muslin sheet. Finer or heavier fabrics may be included, but they should not be as fine as organdy or as heavy as upholstery fabric. Solids, prints, stripes, plaids, even large-patterned fabrics are suitable, depending upon the pattern you choose. Used fabrics in good condition are fine.

Sorting all the fabric by color helps you to see what colors should predominate or what colors you need to add. If you have a lot of two or three colors, you may wish to choose a pattern that has a strong color scheme. If your colors cover the rainbow, a more random pattern might be more suitable.

If you are buying all new fabric, you need only choose a pattern and buy the colors you will need. The choice of quilt patterns is almost endless. Their names read like a history of America, and even a geography: Storm at Sea, Prairie Star, Boston Common, New York Beauty, Clay's Choice, Star of the West, Ohio Rose, Martha's Vineyard, Bluegrass, Log Cabin, Ocean Wave, Ground Breaking, Turkey Track, Twisted Cable, Chimney Sweep, Pineapple, Double Wedding Ring, Grandmother's Garden, Rail Fence, Dolly Madison's Star — all evoke scenes of other days.

The pattern given here, Pointed Star, was chosen for its simplicity and for its adaptability. It makes into a beautiful quilt done in either a coordinated two- or three-colored scheme or in all random colors. It has many variations and you can change it to make a more intricate pattern, or change its size (Fig. 7-2).

The effect can be that of a star, a sunburst or chevrons, depending upon the colors used and their sequence. The diamonds can be all one color for a sunburst, alternating dark and light for a star (Fig. 7-3), in pairs for chevrons (Fig. 7-4) or in two different striped materials for a geometric effect (Fig. 7-5). The corner squares can be in a different color from the edge triangles to emphasize the block effect with stripes.

Fig. 7-3

Fig. 7-4

Fig. 7-5

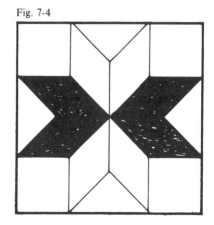

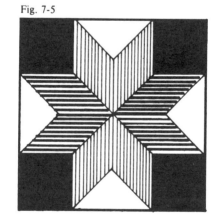

If your available material has small pieces of many different fabrics, each block may have eight different diamonds. In this case, you might wish to give them a more harmonious all-over effect by using some sequence of light and dark colors. Using the sequences mentioned above, treat darks as one color, lights as another. If you do use many different fabrics (and your quilt will be more authentic if you do), it is best to use white for the four squares and four triangles that form the background.

You may cut all the pieces for your quilt at once or do a few blocks at a time. There are advantages to each. Since it is a long-term project, you may come upon some new source or fabric while it is in progress and add new patterns. If you are buying fabric or using a rigid color scheme, you ought to cut your pieces first to be sure you have enough fabric while it is still available.

While such quilts are undoubtedly stunning decorator pieces and were indeed made by our ancestors, the all-one-fabric quilts seem to me less rewarding. A patchwork quilt is after all the epitome of the old Yankee saying, "use it up, wear it out, make it do, or do without." It was from scraps and tidbits that the early ones were made. To create a beautiful work of art, to be passed on for generations, from waste materials with hardly any other use seems to give a reward and a satisfaction unique to quilting.

Before cutting the fabric, trace pattern pieces onto a sheet of medium sandpaper and cut out several pieces of each shape. Be sure to add 1/4-inch seam allowance to every edge when making the pattern. Since you are cutting a large number of pieces, the sandpaper makes a better pattern than paper. A pinned paper pattern makes a lump and leads to uneven cutting; a cardboard pattern slips. But sandpaper is rough enough to grip the fabric and stiff enough to hold its shape. It doesn't have to be pinned to the fabric, which saves you considerable time. Even so, you will probably need more than one of each shape.

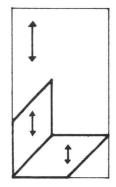

Fig. 7-6 *All pieces should be cut with the grain of the fabric.*

For the pointed star pattern, there are only three shapes: pieces 1-8 (diamonds), 9-12 (triangles) and 13-16 (squares) (Fig. 7-7). For simplicity's sake, we will assume that the triangles and squares will be white, the even numbers of the diamonds will be dark and the odd, light colors.

If you are making a quilt, there will be so many of these little pieces that you need some method for keeping them together, sorted and flat. I thread four needles and make a fat knot in one end of each thread. As I cut squares, I draw a needle and thread through each one once until I have a little stack of squares strung on a thread. I do the same thing with triangles, light diamonds and dark diamonds. When I'm not working with them, I wrap the remaining thread around the stack and stick the needle into the fabric. When it is time to use the pieces, I remove the needle and slip off each patch as I need it. To add more pieces, the needle can be rethreaded.

When cutting pieces, be sure to cut with the grain of the fabric, just

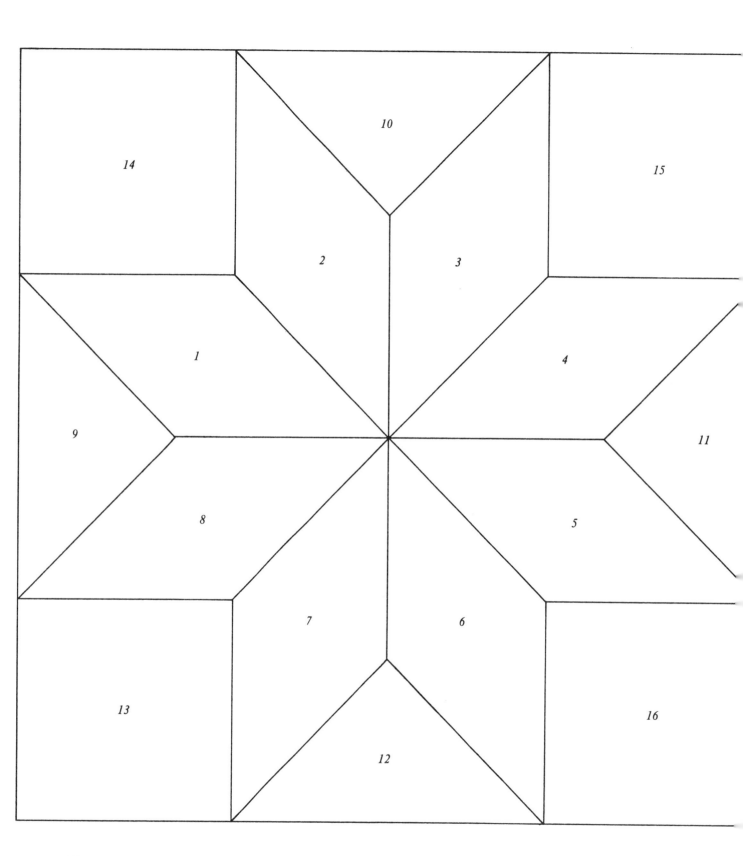

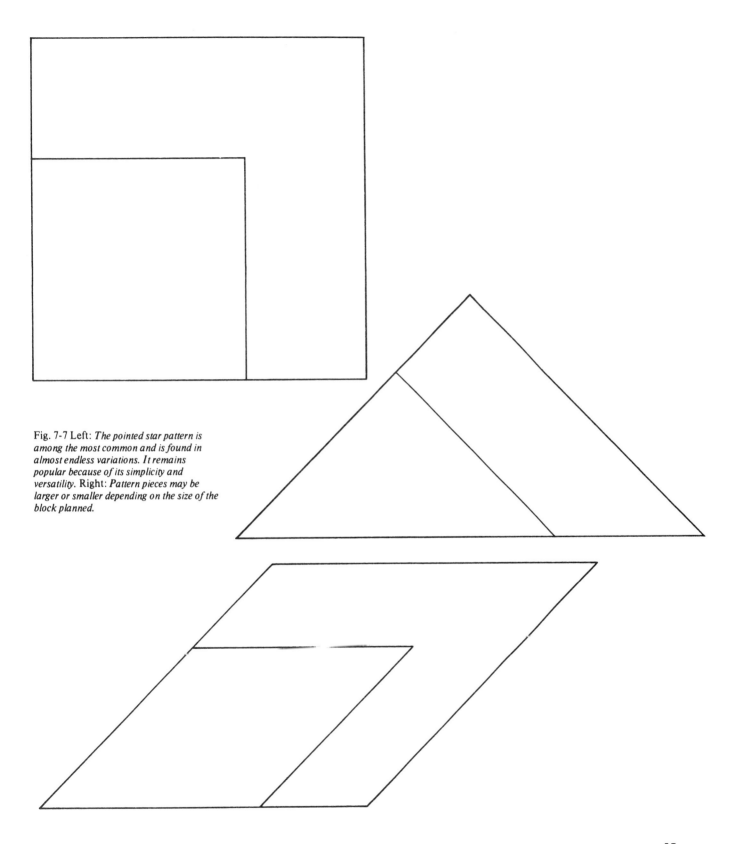

Fig. 7-7 Left: *The pointed star pattern is among the most common and is found in almost endless variations. It remains popular because of its simplicity and versatility.* Right: *Pattern pieces may be larger or smaller depending on the size of the block planned.*

as you would in dressmaking. On scraps you can't tell which is the true grain, but do stay with the direction of the threads. Otherwise the pieces will pull badly when sewn (Fig. 7-6).

To join pieces into blocks, begin with one dark and one light diamond and stitch one side by hand (right sides together, with a 1/4-inch seam), using a single thread and small even stitches. You may pin them if that's easier for you. Then add another diamond, remembering to alternate dark and light, and continue until you have attached all eight in a circle. Before joining the final seam, press the stitched squares to flatten seams. If you cut properly, used 1/4-inch seams and matched all edges as you stitched, you should end up with a perfect star and just enough overlap for the final seam.

If it does not come out right at that point, this is the time to fix the mistake. Check the seams and correct the sources of the problem until the star lies flat. After stitching the final diamond, add the triangles, iron again, and stitch in the corner squares.

Continue making blocks in this way until you have enough for the quilt size you are making. This will depend on whether you plan to attach each starblock directly to the next or separate them with strips of solid color fabric (see page 63).

Whether you are making a large quilt, a baby's quilt or a chair mat consisting of a single block, the method of assembling and quilting is much the same. If you are making a whole quilt, you will need a quilting frame. For a small quilt you can use rug hoops. With a single square, I don't stretch it at all. It is probably better to, and you can make a small frame with four pieces of sturdy but light wood nailed together into a perfect square.

Put down the backing fabric first and thumbtack it to the frame. Lay the batting over this and the pieced square on top. Baste through all layers with long stitches to tack it in place. Using a short, slender needle and #50 thread, single strand, anchor with a knot drawn through from between the layers where it won't show. Quilt all three layers together using tiny stitches 1/8 inch apart, holding the needle straight up and down.

For the pointed star pattern, the best quilting design would be to follow the seams making a row of stitches 1/8 inch inside the seam of each diamond and 1/8 inch away from the diamond seams in each triangle and square. Since the squares are large areas, bisect each with at least a single line of quilting (Fig. 7-8). If you are doing a single square without a frame, work from the center out.

When you have quilted one square, you will readily see why quilting was done at "bees." It was and is a monumental task and one which would take up an entire room in a house for many months if done by one person. Before even considering a quilt, do at least one pillow top or chair seat complete with quilting. Even a good-sized pot holder will give you an idea of the hours involved.

Although the quilting isn't necessary on a patchwork pillow top, it does add greatly to its beauty. Or, if the art of quilting appeals to you

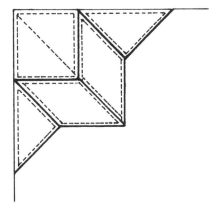
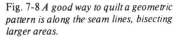
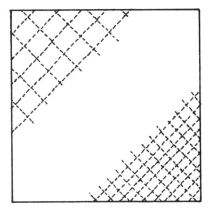

Fig. 7-8 *A good way to quilt a geometric pattern is along the seam lines, bisecting larger areas.*

Fig. 7-9 *A pillow or chair pad can be quilted in a simple grid pattern.*

more than the patchwork, try another old design form, the all-white quilt. This is easily adapted to a pillow top.

Simply replace the pieced top with a plain white fabric of fine weave. With tailor's chalk, or a tracing wheel, mark out a design on the pillow top and quilt it using white thread. The design may be a simple grid of diamonds (Fig. 7-9), or a pineapple (a very common old pattern) or a full-rigged sailing ship, depending upon your ambition. Swirls and curved garlands of leaves were old favorites that could be adapted to an all-white pillow top.

When a quilted piece is completed, it must be bound to cover the raw edges. This is done simply by stitching a strip of fabric along the edge to form a border. If the quilted piece is to be a pillow top, this border is then sewn to the backing. If it is a flat piece like a quilt, pot holder or chair pad, the edge of the binding fabric is sewn onto the face of the piece, then folded over and attached to the back, exactly as bias binding is used in other sewing.

Whether your patchwork and quilting are used in an elegant pot holder or a magnificent quilt, you will have the reward of knowing that you used a method, and probably a pattern, used by women before you since the first settlers arrived. ✹

CHAPTER
8

Victorian Crazy Quilts

Our crazy quilt is a family history, full of memories for us all. It has a piece of velvet from the gown I wore to my first Harvard ball, a piece of silk from the necktie I gave Tim as a high-school graduation gift, a scrap of Thai silk from the dress my mother wore to our wedding.

There are bits and scraps of lace and satins from old dresses and gowns, blue ribbons from the fairs, lace from a long worn-out tablecloth, red velvet from the dress Julie wore her first Christmas. Some of the embroidery was done by friends, and the entire quilt was assembled over cups of warm tea and good conversation with two close friends.

We are a family of scrap savers, so the first task of the quilt was easy. We went through all the trunks and the sewing scraps and Tim's tie rack. Here at last was a home for the beloved silk ties the wrong width or too spotted to wear.

Then we asked friends and family to share. My mother-in-law was moving, and she provided me with bags of scraps from every prom dress Tim's sisters had ever made. One friend brought a bag full of her husband's old neckties; another gave bits of antique ribbon she found in her attic.

Since there were three of us working together, there was soon an ample supply. Variety is important in collecting fabric, and we certainly had a selection.

The next step was to sort it by colors. To make it more manageable, we cut off pieces from large lengths and stored away a lot of bulky ex-

Fig. 8-1 *The rich elegance of crazy-quilt blocks is emphasized by framing them with velvet strips. This quilt took Pat Greene and Mickey Bertera of Keene, New Hampshire, three years to complete.*

tra for future quilts. We pulled old ties apart and pressed them flat and cut flat sections from pieces of clothing. ("Did we ever really wear dresses that length?")

Once cut and sorted, the material was easily stored and quick to bring out and set up for use. Whenever we met, we spread the material out on the dining-room table like a palette from which to choose our colors.

The quilt is made of scraps of material basted and then embroidered onto 14-inch muslin squares. Each finished square will measure 12 inches square when stitched together into the quilt. An old sheet or two will provide ample backing squares.

There are different ways of assembling squares. I start with several "busy" patterned silk scraps and lay them at random on the muslin backing. Then I lay enough other pieces between them to completely cover the muslin. In doing this, remember to have plenty of overlap so the edges of each piece can be turned under.

I view each square as a separate composition — like a painting — and use harmonious colors, contrasting textures and variety of sizes in the pieces of fabric I choose. Once the square is laid out, I pin each piece loosely in the center and begin turning under edges. There should be no raw edges within a square. Sometimes it is best to turn the edges at the ironing board, pressing them under, and then pinning the pieces in place on the muslin as they are done. The outer edges of each square block can be left raw, since they will be covered when the blocks are sewn together into the quilt. Heavy fabrics like velvet that are hard to turn are "bottom pieces," whose raw edges will not be turned, but rather overlaid by surrounding patches of thinner fabrics.

When the square is pressed and pinned, it is ready to be basted. You can skip this step, but I urge you not to. Since every edge must be embroidered, pins will get in the way, stab you and make your work messy. Baste each edge to hold the turned edges in place and press the entire square. It should lie perfectly flat. If it does not, you will have to unbaste and redo it to remove the pucker.

The square is now ready to go in the sewing basket, where it becomes carry-along work. (For years, I was known at town meetings as "the lady with the patchwork quilt.")

The embroidery is, to me, the joy of the whole process. It's all freehand and can be as plain or as fancy as you choose. But each square should have as wide a variety of stitches as possible. The Victorians judged the elegance of their crazy quilts by the number of different kinds of stitches used, as well as by the excellence of their workmanship. Almost any embroidery stitch will do: chain, double chain, outline, spaced rows of stem stitches, feather stitch, buttonhole stitch, cross-stitch, or even rows of French knots. (See Fig. 9-3 for stitch diagrams.)

In addition to the stitches that continue in series, there are those that can be repeated in series. An example of this is a wavy line of stem running stitches in green punctuated by clusters of French knots in red with a green daisy stitch for a leaf here and there. This garland

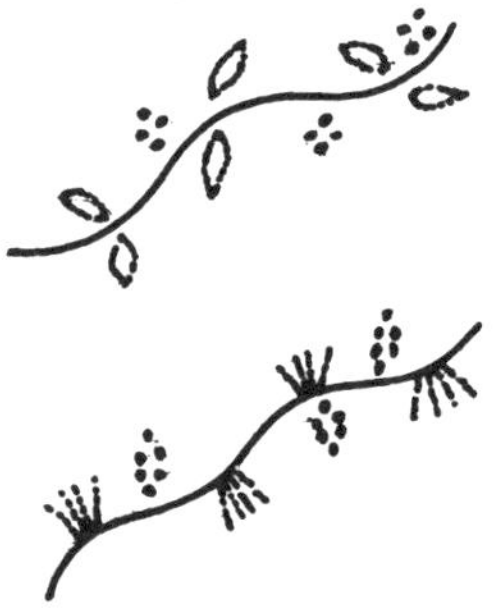

Fig. 8-2a Red French knots with green lazy-daisy and outline stitches combine to make a garland of partridgeberries.
Fig. 8-2b Green straight stitches and brown French knots along a row of outline stitches makes a pine garland.

Deborah Stone Photo

Fig. 8-3 Feather stitches, chevrons, blanket stitches, chains and outline stitches are all good borders. Fabric mementos like this county-fair blue ribbon were often worked into quilts.

Victorian Crazy Quilts

of partridgeberries is almost as fast to do as a feather stitch (Fig. 8-2a).

A brown wavy line of stem stitches with sprays of green straight single stitches and a brown cluster of French knots makes a pine garland (Fig. 8-2b). I have one square (which is my favorite) that has an arbor of grapes complete with tendrils. You wouldn't want to do the whole quilt so elaborately, but it's fun to show off a little on each square.

You can create a great variety of borders just by changing size or proportion of the common stitches and by using a combination of them, such as a line of stem stitches evenly spaced over a row of cross stitches of a different color (Fig. 8-3).

Along with the necessary border embroidery which serves to hold down the edges, Victorian quilts also have embroidered pictures in the plain squares, especially those of velvet. Sprays of flowers, birds, sunbursts, even names or dates can be stitched on velvets for a beautiful rich effect (Fig. 8-4).

In doing our quilts, we found that we forgot what stitches we had used before and tended to get into ruts. One square would have several varieties of chain or blanket (buttonhole) or feather. We solved this by keeping a paper in our basket with new stitches or combinations either listed or drawn so we could refer to it when inspiration failed us.

In Vermont, the Bennington Museum has some fine examples of crazy quilts, and the amount and variety of embroidered decoration on some of them is astonishing. Some borders were an inch wide with row upon row of different stitches. We preferred a simpler style, but drew on many of the ideas we found there.

Once the embroidery is done, it will hold the square together, so the basting can be removed. The square should then be pressed smooth and packed away flat until the other blocks are completed.

The number of square blocks you will need depends on the size of the quilt and on the method you plan to use in joining them together. The traditional crazy quilt was made by putting all the squares together so that the borders of each block melted into the overall jumble. This method takes sixty-three squares for a double-bed quilt, nine by seven feet.

We chose a less common style of assembly which, I think, shows the squares off with more elegance. This involves placing three-inch strips of dark velvet between the squares, so that each is framed and separate.

Assembling the quilt this way is a lot of work, but you will need fewer squares; you will need six rows of seven squares, each separated by velvet, or a total of forty-two squares (see Fig. 8-5). These long rows are then sewn to velvet strips the length of the quilt. The velvet strips should be cut 4-1/2-inches wide to allow generous 3/4-inch seams on each side. The entire quilt is then bordered with a four-inch band of velvet (mitred at each corner).

As the quilt is assembled, the squares must be kept perfectly

Fig. 8-4 *The beautifully embroidered designs found on antique quilts are an inspiration to modern quilt makers.*

Fig. 8-5 *Quilt blocks are alternated with velvet strips to form the finished quilt top. The border is mitred at the corners.*

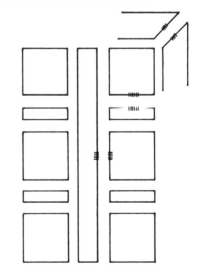

straight. I find it helpful to make a 12-inch square cardboard template and trace around it with a pencil on the muslin side of each block. The pencil line serves as a stitching guide (Fig. 8-6).

Since the silk and satin crazy quilts were usually not quilted (quilting would ruin the effect of the embroidery), but tied, the finishing is relatively easy. Stitch the entire quilt top to a backing the same size, right sides together. Turn, and press the edges lightly. Press velvet face down on a piece of extra velvet to preserve the nap.

In choosing a backing material, remember that the traditional silks and velvets will be both expensive and more difficult to work with. A fine-grained cotton fabric of a color that blends well with the quilt might be a better choice.

After the backing is joined to the quilt top, the entire quilt should be tied, or "tacked." To do this, lay the quilt out perfectly flat on an ironed sheet, using its corners as a guide to keep the quilt corners square. Pin lightly in the seams at the corners between the blocks. Once the blocks are so pinned, you can move the quilt to a tabletop, but be careful — it's like carrying a porcupine!

Make a tack with four-strand embroidery floss in each corner of each block, drawing the thread through and back again, and tying the ends together firmly. Trim the ends to about 1/4 inch. Tacking keeps the quilt top in place and keeps it square.

You can put a batted filling in a silk crazy quilt, but it's not a good

Deborah Stone Photo

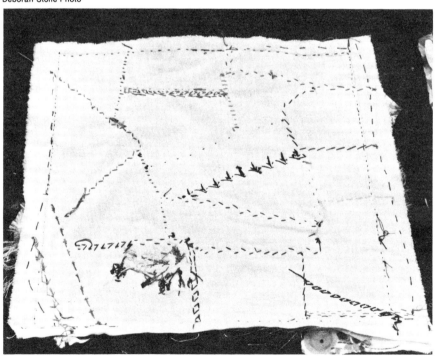

Fig. 8-6 *The back of this block shows how the embroidery actually holds the patches in place. Note the even row of tiny handstitches that join the block to the surrounding velvet, and the pencilled line for stitching guide.*

Victorian Crazy Quilts

Fig. 8-7 *A single block framed and backed with velvet and stuffed makes a handsome pillow.*

Deborah Stone Photo

idea. The fabric and design are not suited to quilting. And since these were (and are) showpieces, they are not washable and are meant to be used as bedspreads and folded over the quilt rack when the bed is in use. The warmth of quilt batting is therefore unnecessary.

If you would like to try your hand at crazy quilting, but don't want to make a whole quilt, the squares make elegant pillows. One 12-inch square with a three- or four-inch velvet border framing it is a perfect size. The backing should be of the same velvet as the border.

In doing just one square, you can have a definite color scheme, and carry it out with the bordering velvet. I did one in shades of green and crimson with some gold tones for highlight and "framed" it in crimson velvet.

To make the border, cut a piece of velvet 20 inches square. Cut an 11-inch square out of the center. Make 1/2-inch cuts diagonally into the corners, and turn under the 1/2-inch of velvet on the inside of the frame (see Fig. 8-7). Place this over the completed crazy-quilt block and baste in place. Check the measurements to make sure it is square.

Run a row of feather stitch over the velvet, close to the edge, making sure your stitches catch all layers of fabric through to the muslin backing. Use four-ply embroidery floss. When the embroidery is completed, stitch the entire pillow top to a 20-inch square of velvet, right sides together, and turn. Press carefully, stuff the pillow, and close the opening with very discreet overcast stitches.

Quilts, or even pillows, are not made with a stopwatch in hand, but we estimate that each quilt block takes about eight hours to complete. With sixty-three blocks required for a traditional crazy quilt, and forty-two for a velvet framed quilt, it might be over-hasty to promise your daughter one for next Christmas. ✹

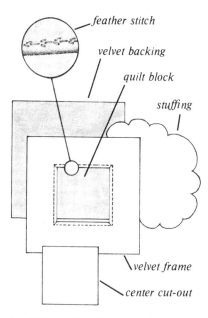

Fig. 8-8 *Assembly of a crazy-quilt pillow.*

How to Embroider Original Crewel Patterns

The art of crewel embroidery was already centuries old when the ladies of the American Colonies used it to decorate their homes. But like many other forms of handwork, crewel changed in the Colonies and began to assume distinctly American characteristics.

Simpler, less busy patterns produced a more airy effect than did the heavily embroidered European ones. Typically, fewer colors were used; entire pieces were even done in monochrome. Samples remain of items embroidered wholly in shades produced by indigo dyes, with stunning effect.

In the cities, stamped linens and a wide variety of colored wools were available, but in more remote areas, patterns were adapted from other decorative crafts, or from a few available patterns shared between households. Some were original freehand drawings.

Likewise, the country women frequently dyed their own wools. The results were often better than the colors of purchased wools — the tones muted and subtle and the shades in much closer series. Even today, many serious embroiderers dye their own wools, using plant dyes for more beautiful and authentic work.

Crewel embroidery had almost disappeared from the repertoire of needle arts until recent interest brought it back into vogue. Now, wools and linens are available once again, and designs are plentiful.

Unfortunately, as happens whenever a craft attains great popularity, some of the material available in kit form is of poor quality and design. But without a stamped pattern and instructions showing

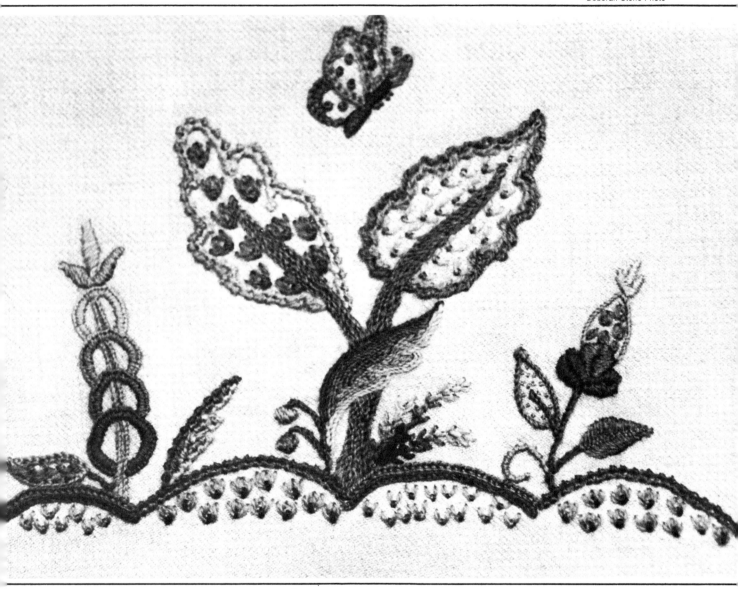

Fig. 9-1 *A small pattern can be very effective worked only in the five values of one color, in this case, old blue.*

Fig. 9-2 *Keep a sampler of stitches on hand to remind you how each is done and how it looks; this is helpful in planning designs.*

which stitch to use where and in what color, it is difficult for the beginner to undertake a project.

With so many excellent patterns now available, it seems a shame to be limited to only those with directions attached. However, it is often difficult to translate a simple line drawing into appropriate stitches. I once did six different versions of a beautiful Queen Anne's lace spray before I found the right stitches.

Entire books can be written (and have been) on the art of crewel embroidery, but very little is available on choosing the right stitches and colors to execute a design. This comes with experience.

The best way to begin is to make a small sampler of the various stitches. This need not be complicated or fancy. A simple scrap of linen twill will do nicely (Fig. 9-2). The only purpose of this sampler is to give you a real picture of the effect of each stitch. For those stitches that are often used in series or in clusters, do both single and multiple stitches. French knots, for example, serve two different purposes when used singly and when used in quantity to cover an area.

You needn't learn every single stitch for your sampler. Begin with the ones you know and add others as you discover them. As you undertake more difficult patterns, new stitches will be needed, but a basic series is enough to begin with.

Traditional crewel designs have a good deal in common in that they tend to follow certain stylized forms originally found in Jacobean needlework. Although modern crewel uses nearly any design, there are those patterns which say "crewel" to us the minute we see them. They are made up of smooth, flowing, curved lines, usually based on floral patterns or other designs from nature.

These designs break down into certain elements that are rearranged in great variety, but remain much the same: leaves, stems, flowers, berries, etc. Some design elements suggest a number of possible stitches, others comparatively few.

In the thistle pattern shown in Fig. 9-4, for example, the round body of the thistle immediately suggests a couched stitch, perhaps a trellis, surrounded by a simple outline stitch, and perhaps a buttonhole stitch reversed so the legs stand outside (Fig. 9-5).

The stem could be any of the line stitches: outline, chain, stem stitch. For roundness I might use two close rows of outline stitch in neighboring values of the same green. The difference in shades would be almost indiscernable, but sufficient to create an illusion of depth.

Any number of stitches could be used for the leaves. They would be effective rendered in rows of closely packed outline stitch in an entire range of values with the darkest at the center forming the vein. Because of the jagged edges, this would be somewhat more difficult than a long and short stitch radiating outward from the vein in increasingly lighter values.

An alternative is to do one half of each leaf in one of the solid fashions above and the other half in a more open design — perhaps with a border of chain or satin stitch filled with random cross or seed stitches inside. The vein could be a simple outline stitch in the darkest

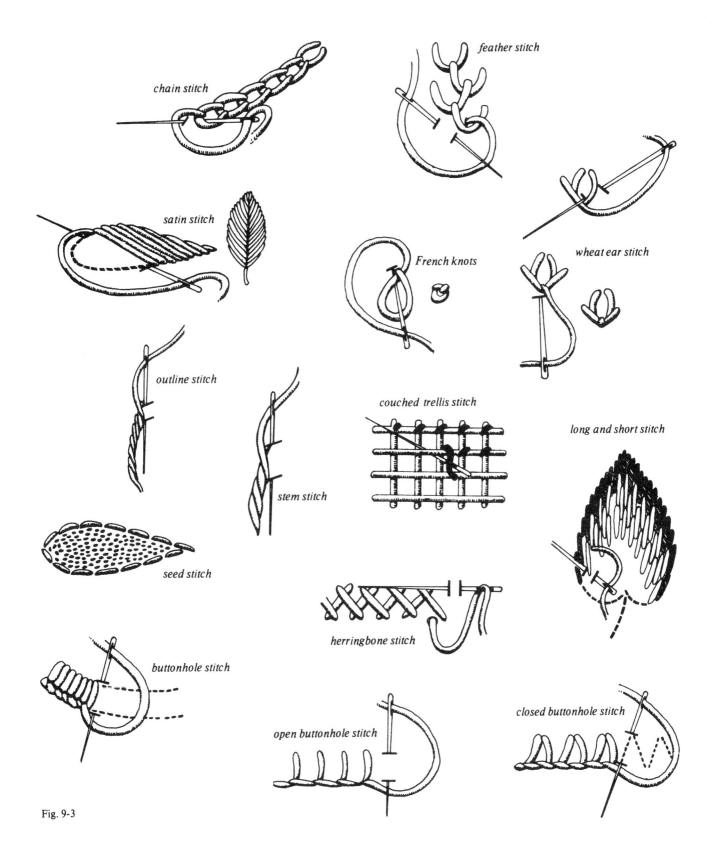

chain stitch

feather stitch

satin stitch

French knots

wheat ear stitch

outline stitch

stem stitch

couched trellis stitch

long and short stitch

seed stitch

herringbone stitch

buttonhole stitch

open buttonhole stitch

closed buttonhole stitch

Fig. 9-3

Fig. 9-4 *The thistle pattern, actual size.*

value. Since the pattern is heavily foliage, this last approach could be the best.

The bottom leaf can be done either in the same style as the others or in a different way. Each of its three segments could even be in a different stitch, with the heaviest and darkest at the bottom.

The mound at the base is a good place to show off a little. Its top edge should be of a solid stitch to outline it, but the center could be a loose filler, such as wheat ears or seed stitch. Or buttonhole stitches worked in groups of three to form little triangles could be combined with a perfectly fitted reverse row, tapering toward the ends. If this looks too much like a mouthful of teeth in the colors you've chosen, perhaps it could be outlined in stem stitch and filled with herringbone.

Long and short was often used for mounds in old pieces, but there are so many other places where this stitch is so effective that I save it for flowers, leaves and designs that need its perfection in color blending.

The ideal place to exhibit your skill with long and short is in the top of the thistle. Do the bottom fringe, which is fairly small in the two lightest values, the lightest at the top. Then begin the top fringe, using all but the darkest value, starting again with the lightest at the top. This will give dimension.

How to Embroider Original Crewel Patterns

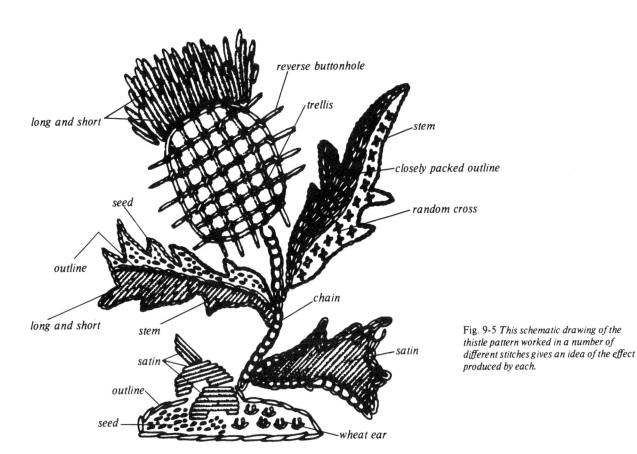

reverse buttonhole

trellis

long and short

stem

closely packed outline

random cross

seed

outline

long and short

stem

chain

satin

satin

outline

seed

wheat ear

Fig. 9-5 *This schematic drawing of the thistle pattern worked in a number of different stitches gives an idea of the effect produced by each.*

Once you have decided on the stitches, you will have an idea of how many colors you need. Perhaps you can determine color and stitches at the same time, but as they involve separate considerations, it is easier to think about one at a time.

Begin with the central design element — in this case, the body of the thistle. Decide what color you want it to be. Don't be limited to its color in nature. If you want an old rose thistle, or a gold one, by all means have one! Because I like the muted colors best, I might choose an old blue, but a true blue or purple would do as well.

We spoke of values in discussing the choice of stitches earlier. Each color in crewel yarn has five values which are numbered from 1 to 5, #1 being the lightest, #5 the darkest. These values are so close that when used in sequence they appear to blend like mixed paint. This is especially true when they are used in a stitch like long and short, which simply facilitates this blending.

There are several ways to use the thistle color once you have chosen it. You can use one value throughout, perhaps #4, for the trellis and use another value, probably #2, for the couching. Another possibility is to lay all the vertical trellis lines first in value #3, then lay the horizontal ones, using two each of #2, #3 and #4, with #4 at the bottom. The couching could be in #1 or #5, or in the same shade as the horizontal lines.

Fig. 9-6 *Another classic crewel pattern that can be worked in many different ways.*

If you decide to use only one value in the trellis, you might round out the design by varying the value in the couching, using the darker values around the edges and the lighter ones in the center. Or you could use a contrasting color, perhaps old gold, to do the couching, again varying values for dimension.

The top of the thistle is next. Since the design has only four basic elements, you might wish to make this crown a different color. If you chose blue or purple, old gold might be good, or rose. If you have made the globe of the thistle in varying shades, you could even make the crown in the same color, since you have created variety enough to keep it from looking flat. If you do this, you will definitely want to make the couching in a contrasting color.

Once you have chosen the colors for your thistle, gather a bundle of skeins, or several looped strands, in your hand like a nosegay. Include every color and value you will be using. To this bouquet add "foliage" of skeins of green. Use a bundle of all values, trying each green in turn until you find the one that is best suited to the other colors chosen.

Once you have selected your green, you need only decide what to do about the mound. Since the green is all in the middle, and the thistle takes up the top, it would be a good idea to incorporate one of the accent colors from the top into the mound.

If you used gold at all, the choice is easy. If you didn't, you have to decide whether to add a new color, probably brown or dark gold, into your scheme. It might be best to do so, just for the variety it would provide.

If you add golden brown without having used it at the top of the

How to Embroider Original Crewel Patterns

design, best combine it in some way with the green. You could do the top of the mound in gold or brown, and the bottom or center in your green. This provides more balance and draws the design together into one unit instead of three separate ones. You could also introduce brown or deep gold by doing the stem with one row of green and one row of gold or brown.

Admittedly, it is easier to plan colors for a small design than for a large, complex one. But the same techniques are used in creating a harmonious and balanced picture. Intense colors should be distributed evenly throughout the design; colors which are predominant in one area should be picked up as accents in other areas to unify the work.

The second pattern given (Fig. 9-6) is for you to experiment with. It has more separate elements, but some suggestions are already in the drawing to help you in planning. The seed stitches and French knots shown in the leaf can be used or ignored. You can also vary the design in any way you like. Make the berry near the base into an acorn, or a group of small berries, or change the shape of smaller leaves. Enlarge the pattern to fit a larger piece.

As you choose stitches, refer to your sampler, and for each element pick the stitch whose effect is closest to the real thing. Cluster flowers like Queen Anne's lace are best represented in French knots, smooth petals in satin or long and short. Use your imagination: you have more colors, more patterns, and better fabrics available to you than the Colonial housewife did, and your work can be just as fine and just as original as hers. ✹

Deborah Stone Photo

Fig. 9-7 *A larger Queen Anne's lace can be done with raised rose stitch as well as French knots.*

CHAPTER 10

Cross-Stitch Samplers

Samplers were once exactly what their name implied: a sample of a seamstress's work and skill. The stitches in a sampler were added as each was perfected, and the finished example was there for reference in future embroidery.

Later on in the Colonies, the sampler became a teaching tool as well as a record of stitches. Girls learned their alphabet and numbers by embroidering them on a sampler. Pictures and patterns and a bit of verse decorated the remaining areas, with finer work as the maker's age and skill increased.

More recently a sampler has come to mean a cross-stitched verse or epigram to frame, often with a picture along the bottom or border.

The art of cross-stitch, which is now so often executed in large stitches over a stamped pattern, was once a fine and intricate form of embroidery. Tiny, perfectly even crosses were made by counting threads, and they were worked so closely that they formed solid lines suitable for embroidering letters in many different scripts.

Although we often think of cross-stitch as a separate form of embroidery, it was originally used in combination with other stitches. Cross-stitch was used for alphabets and borders on samplers, while other stitches formed scenes, patterns and filler designs.

Whether used by itself or in combination with others, cross-stitch has a charm of its own. It is particularly useful in embroidering mottos, quotations and names and is therefore a good choice for framed pieces. Smaller items, such as pincushions, glasses cases, evening

Fig. 10-1 *Lucy Barrett was ten years old in 1795, when she stitched this magnificent sampler. (Courtesy Museum of the Concord Antiquarian Society, Concord, Massachusetts.)*

Cross-Stitch Samplers

purses and embroidered bookmarks may also be created from cross-stitch.

In planning projects for fine counted thread work, it is best to stay with small items that do not get heavy wear, since there is considerable background fabric which will soil easily. Although it may be used as decorative trimming on clothes, it is only suitable for certain fabrics and should not be used on clothes subject to frequent washing. Large cross-stitch is better there.

There are two ways to do fine cross-stitch. One is to use a fine, evenly woven linen with a definite weave (not too close) — Hardanger or Aïda cloth — and count threads. This is not as difficult as it sounds, since each cross covers two threads in each direction. By charting the pattern on graph paper first, you can easily see where the next stitch goes. Each square on the graph equals two threads, or one cross-stitch.

The other way, which is how complicated designs were done many years ago, is to use a material called cross-stitch canvas. This looks like a very thin needlepoint canvas. The threads are very evenly, but loosely, woven, and the material is quite stiff. A piece of this canvas is placed over the linen and basted lightly in place. The cross-stitches are then made right over the threads — it is like having the graph paper right on the linen. When the embroidery is completed, you snip the threads of the canvas and pull them out from under the stitches. What is left is perfectly even cross-stitching on clean linen.

Fig. 10-2 *Simple cross-stitch patterns to use alone or work into larger designs.*

Fig. 10-3 *An alphabet adapted to cross-stitch.*

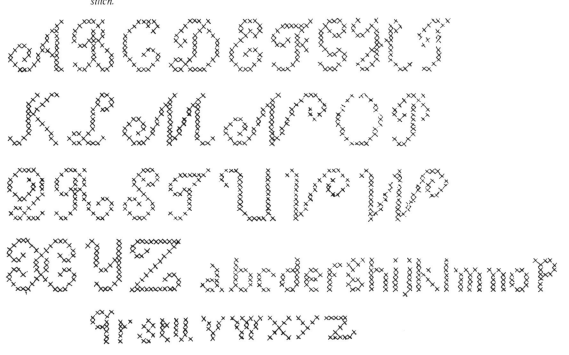

The current popularity of needlepoint has made it easy for cross-stitch embroiderers to find patterns. Any charted needlepoint pattern can be used for cross-stitch. But bear in mind that the two are separate arts and have their own strengths and weaknesses.

While needlepoint covers the entire canvas, cross-stitch has linen background. Also, the subtle shading available in needlepoint wool is not to be found in embroidery floss. The very nature of cotton thread prevents it from blending subtly as wool does. The cotton colors are livelier and more vibrant. So choose simpler designs using contrasting colors that show off the brilliance of the cotton floss. (Alphabets, however, are done exactly the same in needlepoint and cross-stitch.)

When you have chosen designs and alphabets you like, sketch the design roughly on white paper of the same size as the finished piece you plan to make. By folding the paper in quarters and into quarters again, you have it broken into sections which make centering much easier.

When you have your rough design the way you want it, go over its outlines in black ink and place fine graph paper over the sketch. With pencil, trace the placement of the design units — the perimeters of the lettered section, the borders, etc.

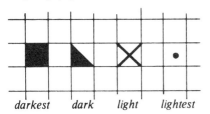

Fig. 10-4 *By using symbols for light and dark colors, you can even indicate shading on your graph pattern.*

darkest   dark   light   lightest

Remove the graph and color your rough sketch using colored pencils. This gives you a chance to see the colors as they will finally appear, since colors on the blue paper look much different.

Using your colored sketch and the charted patterns for counting, make your final pattern on the graph paper. For this, I use a series of colored felt-tip writing pens. Since you are doing cross-stitch, not needlepoint, these colors will suffice. If you wish to distinguish between a light green and dark green, for example, mark over the green dot of one with your yellow pen to lighten it. The colors will mix just enough for you to distinguish the difference. For several shades, use a key system with different markings. This requires a steady hand and a fine point on the felt pen, however (Fig. 10-4).

When you have completed your pattern, you are ready to embroider. Cut your linen about an inch larger all around than your finished project will be to allow for finishing. Stitch around the edges with whipstitch or a zigzag machine to prevent ravelling, since the material will receive considerable handling. Mark the center lines at the edges of the linen in tailor's chalk, or make little tacks of tied thread to help you center the pattern on the fabric.

Because each linen is a different weave, you will have to experiment on a scrap to see how many strands of floss you will use for your crosses. Make a series of sample crosses over two threads (three if the linen is very fine), or use a scrap of embroidery canvas over your linen sample.

Try crosses made of two, three, four, five and six strands of floss for comparison. Choose the example that covers the fabric evenly and fully without making a great fat lump. Use this number of strands for your embroidery.

Where you begin is up to you. I begin at the very center and work

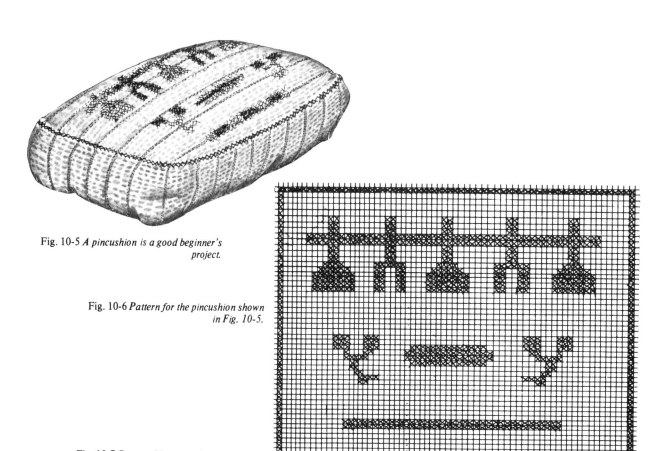

Fig. 10-5 *A pincushion is a good beginner's project.*

Fig. 10-6 *Pattern for the pincushion shown in Fig. 10-5.*

Fig. 10-7 *Reversed hearts make an attractive border design with many variations. They may be done either in outline as shown or filled in, or stitched in alternating colors.*

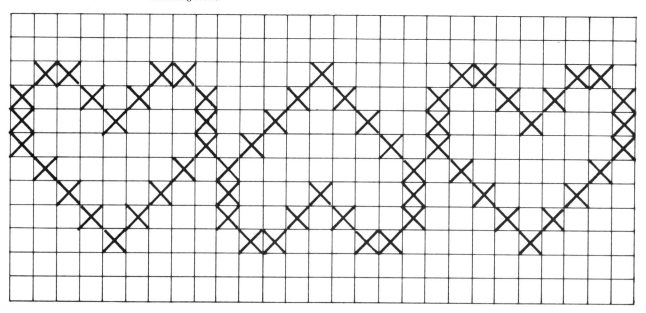

outward, but most embroiderers begin at the top and work down. Remember that you are embroidering, not writing, so you don't have to work the overall pattern from left to right. It helps to work each design segment from left to right, however, since your cross-stitches should be in even rows with as little doubling back as possible.

Whether or not you use embroidery hoops is up to you as well. I don't find them necessary when the stitches are so fine, but anyone who is accustomed to them will have trouble without them. I do use a small thimble.

To save threading and rethreading, I keep a palette of needles all threaded with the different colors. If you can avoid it, don't make knots. Begin with a very small one in each design section if you must, but thereafter, draw an inch of thread through a row of existing stitches.

I was taught embroidery by my mother, who is a perfectionist about handwork, and later by an expert embroiderer who judged the quality of the work by turning it over. Good work should be just as neat on the back as on the front, she insisted, and she tolerated no tags or loose ends hanging out. Since her work is pictured in the most authoritative works on embroidery, I never argued with her!

Before embarking on the monumental task of a sampler, it is well to test your skill on a smaller piece, perhaps suitable for a small gold desk frame or the top of a dress-pin cushion for a bureau.

The patterns given here (Figs. 10-2, 10-6 and 10-7) are suitable for either. A very simple pattern to begin with is the border of hearts around two initials. Hearts, crosses, or any other symmetrical designs are easy to do in sequence, since after the first one, you don't have to count stitches. You can tell by looking at your work how many crosses there should be in each row.

Once you have completed your embroidery, finish the project as you would any other sewn work. Make the pincushion top into a miniature pillow by stitching it to a back of the same linen or a velveteen that matches a predominant color in the embroidery. Tassels are easily made by making a bundle of threads, tying them together with another thread at the top and knotting the entire bundle right under the top (see Fig. 10-8). Trim the ends even and sew the tassels to the corners by the original tying thread at the top.

You can make four tassels by cutting a new skein of embroidery floss in half without separating the coils. Then divide each end into two equal sections and tie as above. This saves a lot of work

To finish a sampler, cut a piece of cardboard 1/8 inch smaller than the frame. Center your linen on it and fold the edges over it. I catch them with long stitches back and forth across the cardboard to hold it firm. When the backing is on the frame, these will be hidden. ✸

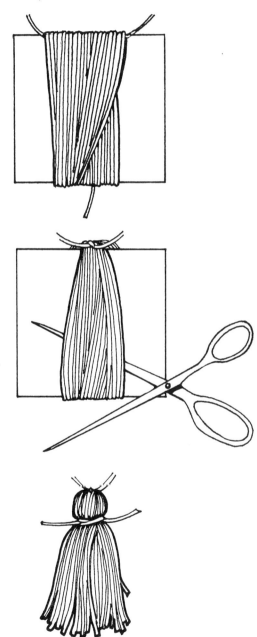

Fig. 10-8 *Tassels are made from matching embroidery thread.*

CHAPTER 11

Swedish Weaving
(Huck Towel Embroidery)

Different fabrics and weaves suggest different needlework styles, and the closely woven huck toweling is a natural for its own special style of embroidery.

Along the length of the bolt runs a series of double threads which stand out above the rest of the weave in even, staggered rows. These are perfect for just catching the embroidery threads run through them. The effect is that of a perfect row of running stitch. By skipping back and forth from row to row, perfect zigzag, flame, Greek-key, dovetail and other patterns can be formed.

Although it was used primarily for borders on towels, this form of embroidery has also been worked in wools, forming all-over patterns for pillow tops. From a distance it almost resembles bargello in its effect. By using embroidery floss and working in a lighter style with an overall pattern, the effect is that of fine weaving.

Since the top threads alone are used for anchoring the embroidery, no threads show on the back. To keep the needle from penetrating the fabric by mistake, I use a tapestry needle — the same one I use for needlepoint. But a regular embroidery needle will do just as well.

Begin with a simple border on a towel. Use however many strands of embroidery floss you like — all six will make a bold design, three a more delicate one. Run a straight row of thread the whole width of the towel, catching it under each of the raised threads. Make this row about three or four inches from the hem of the towel.

Use this row of stitches as a center and repeat subsequent rows of

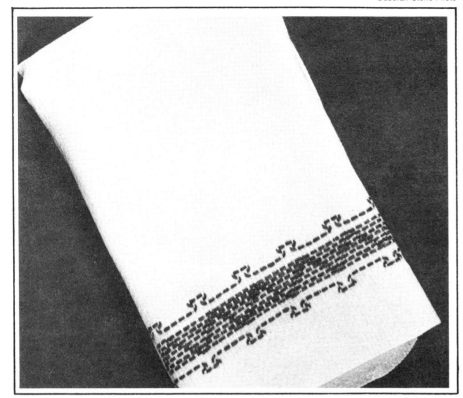

Fig. 11-1 *A tea towel embroidered in blue linen thread on a fine-weave hucking shows one of the many borders possible.*

different stitches on either side of it until the border is the width you like (Fig. 11-2). Each row can be a different design or stitch, or several rows of the same thing can be worked in succession to form an overall pattern. By skipping from row to row and by doubling back, even looping through existing rows, interesting designs can be made.

A narrow stripe can be made, for example, by picking up each thread in two adjoining rows. Since the rows are staggered, this produces a narrow zigzag. By skipping two rows, the zigzag can be made into a wider band, and by using only alternate threads it can be made into a larger design. This is attractive if used for several rows in succession.

A common stitch in Swedish weaving is the dovetail, made by picking up four threads in one row, then moving several rows down, and two rows backwards, picking up four more, returning to the first row and using the next four threads so that each thread in each row has been used. The result resembles dovetailing in furniture.

A variation of this loops the embroidery floss through the corner of the previous dovetail, forming a loose chain. Don't be afraid to go through the threads from the wrong direction causing loops and twists; in fact, the latter are a distinctive characteristic of Swedish weaving.

For example, a looped version of the zigzag goes through each thread with the needle facing the work already done, instead of forward. This forms a curved double-crossed effect that looks something

Fig. 11-2 *Additional rows may be added until the border is as wide as you wish.*

Swedish Weaving (Huck Towel Embroidery)

Fig. 11-3 *These bordered towels were created by Patricia Schatz of The Huckery, Malverne, New York.*

Fig. 11-4 *A child's poncho and skirt set by Patricia Schatz of The Huckery. This traditional Christmas-tree design would also be attractive on towels for the holidays.*

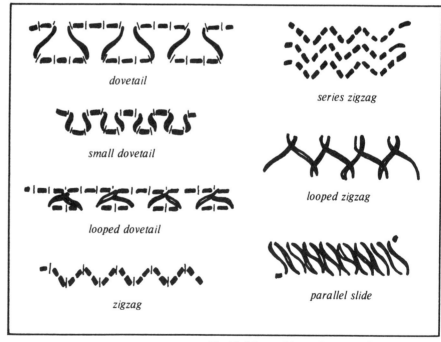

dovetail

small dovetail

looped dovetail

zigzag

series zigzag

looped zigzag

parallel slide

Fig. 11-5 *Some of the stitches used in Swedish weaving.*

Swedish Weaving (Huck Towel Embroidery)

like the herringbone stitch in regular embroidery. By varying the distance between stitches, the line can be very loose or tightly packed.

The best way to make up a new stitch is to take a scrap of huck toweling — an old towel works fine — and experiment. If you get something you like, you have a sample of it whenever you need inspiration. If you don't like it, just leave it — you may think of a variation on it that you do like. Keep this sampler to work from in the future.

If different colors are used, rows can be overlapped with a beautiful effect. The dovetail pattern done in two different-colored rows, the second directly beneath the first, will appear to be interlocked.

Rows of different stitches in different colors can be used one on top of the other, too. For example, if you do a pattern that involves a wide band with long stitches, you can anchor these in the middle with another row of a very simple design in another color. A very wide dovetail or zigzag might be highlighted and, at the same time, anchored with a straight line through the middle, over the long, loose stitches.

Although white or ecru is the traditional fabric color, huck toweling is available in rich, dark colors, too. These are stunning worked in all-white patterns. Here is a place to show off your most dramatic designs, since the contrast will accent them. Black or dark brown is a good color to use on gold, especially if these colors dominate in your kitchen.

For me, the fun of Swedish weaving is that instead of following a pattern, you make up your own. Each piece is original, and each piece is uniquely yours. ✹

Decorating Furniture with False Graining, Striping, and Marbling

Even in the days when antiques were new, furniture was not always made of the finest or most beautiful woods. Cabinetmakers invented a number of ways to either camouflage or embellish the woods they had at hand.

False graining, originally devised to make common woods simulate rarer or more expensive ones, soon became a finish in its own right and an art in itself. It is doubtful that false graining even fooled anyone — or indeed ever was meant to — but as a decorative finish it was very popular in Victorian days, and was often combined with painted or stenciled designs and striping.

Briefly, the false-grained finish consists of an opaque undercoat sealed with shellac or varnish and a second coat of another color or shade applied over the first in a thin streaky manner to simulate the whorls and striations of wood grain. The undercoat color depends on the type of wood being simulated, but is usually some shade of yellow, red or brown.

False-grained and other opaque finishes were particularly important in the manufacture of chairs, which were frequently made out of more than one wood. Legs were beech or other hardwood that took turning well, while the seat was easier to shape in pine. This combination, of course, resulted in an unmatched chair, and an opaque finish was needed to mask the difference in woods.

In this discussion of false graining, we are not talking about forgery — the attempt to make one wood look like another in order to mislead. We are talking about a form of decoration. So when

Fig. 12-1 *False graining done many years ago decorates this lyre-back chair being readied for recaning.*

rosewood, for example, is mentioned as a wood to simulate, the actual wood itself serves only as a reference point for colors and grain. False-grained rosewood will not look like the real thing; rather, it will look like a stylized imitation.

The directions that follow are for doing (or redoing) an entire piece. If you have a piece of furniture with its decoration showing just a little, localized damage, but generally in good condition otherwise, you can touch it up using the techniques outlined below. But in that case, it is imperative to use the identical method and materials to repair the damage in order to achieve a good match to the rest of the piece.

The rosewood finish is one of the most elegant false grainings and is often used on chairs to be stenciled. Let's assume that you have such a chair, and that you have first stripped off all the old finish and sanded the chair smooth.

Now mix together two parts turpentine, two parts Japan drier, and one part Venetian red tinting color. (Tinting colors are available from craft suppliers.) Paint the chair, wiping off any excess. The chair should be evenly stained. Let it dry 24 hours — longer in very damp weather.

For a rosewood finish (only), it is not necessary to seal the undercoat with shellac or varnish. When the undercoat has dried, wipe the surface lightly to remove any paint dust. Thin flat black enamel with turpentine until the paint is the consistency of milk. Working on one area at a time (one slat, one rung, etc.), paint on a small amount of black, and then immediately wipe across it lightly with a crumpled paper towel for larger areas, or a dry paint brush for tight places and joints. The object is to wipe off enough black to let the red show through in streaks. The temptation is to get the streaks too even. Wiggle the brush or towel slightly and vary the angle of the brush for variety. Wipe with the direction of the wood grain when you can see it. The grain will be lengthwise on rungs, slats and stretchers. On chests, it will be top-to-bottom on sides and edges, and across on tops and drawer fronts.

As you work, if you don't like the results in an area, simply wipe off the top paint with a rag and start again. If you plan to stencil the main (top) back slat, paint it a solid flat black. Other areas which will carry small stenciled designs, such as the side posts and the front of the chair seat, should be false-grained.

Before your first attempt at false graining, borrow a piece that has already been done, or at least study one thoroughly. It does help to have an example of how the finished product should look (Fig. 12-1).

Let the chair dry 24 hours, and it is ready to stencil (see p. 38). If you are stenciling, or after the stenciling is done, cover the entire piece with one coat of clear varnish. If there is any striping to be done, do it here, after the first coat of varnish has dried. Then give the chair one coat of glossy clear varnish and two coats of eggshell clear varnish.

Striping is a very easy thing to do unless you get nervous about

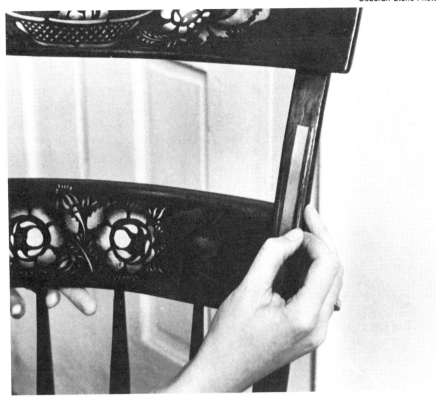

Fig. 12-2 *Striping is easiest to do along edges where you can use your finger as a guide.*

doing it, in which case your hand will shake and ruin it. You will need a striping brush, which can be purchased, or which can be made very simply, as follows. Snip a dozen or so hairs out of a real-bristle (not plastic-bristle) paint brush. The hairs should be at least two inches long. Tie them in a bunch with heavy thread to the end of a toothpick or matchstick. If the bristles are more than three inches long, give them a haircut to that length, cutting evenly across.

On most furniture, and especially on rosewood-finish chairs, striping is done in a yellow made from equal parts of chrome yellow and yellow ochre artist's oil paint, dulled slightly with raw umber. Thin with turpentine to heavy-cream consistency. Dip the brush into the paint up to the top of the bristles, and brush some of the paint off along the side of the paint container.

Until you learn to judge exactly how much paint you need to make an even line, make a short stroke on a piece of paper first to be sure your brush isn't overloaded. To paint, hold the brush at a low angle and let the bristles drag along, leaving paint as they drag. This fills in and straightens the line as you paint (Fig. 12-2).

Striping that goes along the edge of a piece is the easiest, since you can run your little finger along the edge as a guide. Stop at the corners, leaving a gap, and do all the straight sides first. Then go back to the corners and complete the curves, holding the brush upright so the bristles won't drag and widen the line in the curve; continue to follow

Decorating Furniture with False Graining, Striping, and Marbling

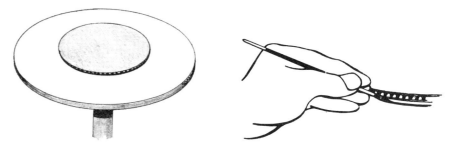

Fig. 12-3 *Where the striping must be some distance away from an edge, a cardboard template makes an excellent guide.*

the line of the edge with your finger.

If you make a mistake, rub it off and start again. That's why you varnished first. Keep a small, flat artist's brush, clean and dry, to pick up unwanted paint or straighten a wiggly edge. If you are striping where there is no edge near enough to follow, tape a yardstick or foot ruler about an inch away and follow that with your finger. If you are attempting an oval border around a stenciled or painted design on a table or bureau top, cut a template of heavy cardboard that will fit about an inch within the stripe you plan to paint, tape it in place, and follow its edge with your finger as you stripe (Fig. 12-3).

Besides rosewood, there are many other false grains. Lighter examples are found where the base coat is a cream, tan, or yellow, with darker shades used for the overlay. For this type of false graining, paint the entire piece with the lighter color in a flat oil-base (never latex) paint. Let this undercoat dry, and seal with a coat of clear shellac. (Note that this sealing step is not necessary for the rosewood finish.)

Mix an oil-base paint in a darker color. One way to do this is to add raw umber to the color you used for the base coat. Paint the darker

Deborah Stone Photo   Fig. 12-4 *Marbling requires only a feather and an unsteady hand.*

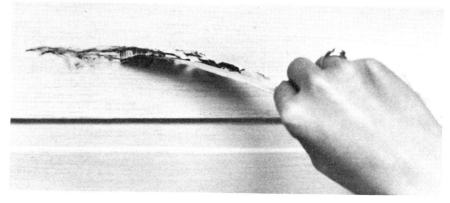

Decorating Furniture with False Graining, Striping, and Marbling

color on and wipe it off as for the rosewood finish. Since the colors are lighter than the red and black used in rosewood, the grain you design will be more visible. In addition to the paper towel and dry brush, you can use a natural sponge, an old beat-up paint brush, or even a pocket comb for graining. All make interesting, stylized grains. If the graining appears too harshly contrasted to the base, you can soften the edges of the graining effects with a dry, fine-bristled paint brush.

And, of course, if you don't like the effect at all, you can always wipe it off and begin again. The oil-base paint won't penetrate the shellac coating with which you sealed the base.

Another decorative technique, often used in the past on bureau or table tops, and also on wall paneling, is marbling. This has an elegant Victorian look and is surprisingly easy to do.

First, strip and sand the wooden surface and seal with three coats of shellac, smoothing the finish with fine steel wool after each coat has dried.

Next, paint the entire surface with white enamel thinned with two tablespoons of turpentine to the pint. Cover the surface as smoothly and quickly as you can. Thin half a cup of gray, tan or dull pink enamel with a tablespoon of turpentine. Dip a turkey (or goose or duck) feather about a foot long into the colored enamel and make a thin wavering line on the wet paint (Fig. 12-4). Every so often, rotate the feather to one side or the other, but don't do it in a regular pattern. You want some big wiggles, some small ones, some closely spaced, and some far apart. It helps if you have a piece (or a picture) of real marble to look at.

Experiment a little first on a prepared board until you get the idea. Unlike striping, marbling does not require a steady hand. In fact, it's better if you don't have one. You can cover the finished marbling when dry with clear shellac, but it isn't necessary.

If you are touching up an old piece with any of these techniques, remember that wet paint and dry paint are shades apart. Experiment on a sample piece of wood and let your work dry at least 24 hours before judging the match. When you get the right colors, simply prepare the damaged area by smoothing with steel wool to bevel the rough edges of the old paint, so that your own paint job will blend into the original.

Some beautiful effects can be achieved with these old finishes, and their study can become a fascinating hobby, as well as a means of restoring antique treasures. ✸

CHAPTER

13

Making Brooms

$\mathbf{T}$here are few things more satisfying than making a useful house-hold tool, especially if you make it from materials you have grown yourself. Brooms are especially well suited to home production since they require no special equipment or tools.

Broomcorn was once grown abundantly in Massachusetts, which was a center for broom-making. Old Sturbridge Village now grows a limited quantity of this material, but it can be grown easily anywhere that sweet corn grows.

Its name is misleading, for although it grows on a tall stalk and has a tassel, it is not corn, but a relative of sorghum and millet. Its grow-ing habits are cornlike, and the best place to plant it is adjacent to your sweet corn, which will afford some protection from the wind to the tall, slender stalks. Cultivation, soil requirements and planting are just like those of corn.

Once you have broomcorn growing, you can save the seed from year to year. You shouldn't plant it near millet or sorghum, however, if you plan to save seed. Plan on about ten row feet for a good-sized broom. That's more than you need, but it will give you a little extra to experiment with.

Growing broomcorn requires little attention beyond occasional hoeing. Toward fall when the heads of seed have formed, but are still green, break the stalk over about 2-1/2 feet from the top. Let the corn dry, hanging like this, for a few days if the weather is nice. Broomcorn mildews easily, so don't let it hang in the field during bad weather. If

Fig. 13-1 *A handmade fireplace broom will last for many years. This one was made at Old Sturbridge Village.*

Fig. 13-2 *Not corn at all, but a sorghum, broomcorn is shown here just short of tassel, from which the broom is made.*

Fig. 13-3 *Pegs set three inches apart at right angles hold the broom in place on the handle.*

Fig. 13-4 *Each stalk of broomcorn looks like a miniature broom itself.*

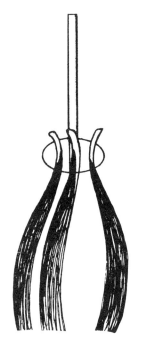

Fig. 13-5 *Pieces of broomcorn are tied securely around the handle.*

you have to cut the corn and take it to shelter, be sure to bring it out into the sun for curing whenever possible. It does need the sun to cure properly. If a rainy spell threatens, it's better to cut the corn, tie it in bundles of two or three and hang it in a dry airy place to dry thoroughly. If you leave it standing on the stalk, the seeds will weigh down the small stems and make them curl; for a good broom, these must be kept straight.

If cut at the right time and cured properly, the straw should be strong, supple and straight. The seeds can be raked out with an old saw blade. This also loosens the straw a little and gives it more bulk.

In order to reduce the bulk around the handle on a full-sized broom, you can shave the stalks down a little, starting about an inch above the tassel. For a hearth broom this is not necessary, and if you plan to weave the top, leave about one-third round.

For a broomstick, use any straight hardwood sapling the size of a common broom (popple* will do, and since it has almost no other use, this is my choice). Peel off the bark and let the sapling dry for a few weeks. If necessary, you can whittle it down to give it better shape or make it smaller, but it's easier to pick the right-sized tree to begin with. You can use an old broomstick or purchase one, but I like to make them myself.

About three inches from the bottom, drill a hole the size of a 1/4-inch dowel and put a 3-1/2-to-4-inch-long dowel through it (if you don't have a dowel stick handy, you can whittle one from a twig very quickly). About three inches above the first dowel, drill a second hole at right angles to the first, and put a peg in it, too (Fig. 13-3).

You can use nails here, but I prefer the dowel pegs. These act as an anchor so the broom won't slide around on the handle and they give you something to brace your work against.

Choose thirty-five good pieces of broomcorn (twenty for a hearth broom) and lay them in the bathtub (or a long trough). Pour boiling water over them and let them soak about 20 minutes, until they are pliable. Or if you have a deep container such as a milk can, fill it with boiling water to the depth of the stalk (the tassel end doesn't have to be wet) and stand the corn in it, cane end down.

Using a stout cotton or linen twine (not a synthetic, which will stretch), tie one layer of cornstalks around the handle (Fig. 13-5). The tops of the corn should be about 15 inches from the bottom of the broom handle. If the overlap is much less, the broom will not be as strong. Tie them in two places.

If you have not already shaved down the stalks, and you are making a full-sized broom, it is a good idea to do it here. This reduces the bulk of the top and makes it look nicer, along with making it easier to handle. Add a second layer of stalks and tie them twice. These ties are temporary. If you are making a full-sized broom, add a third layer.

All brooms are alike to this point. The finishing method depends on your own skill and ambition. The broom may simply be tied at in-

Populus tremuloides, or aspen.

tervals from the point where the stalk turns to tassel to the top of the stalk, or you may weave the corn stalks for a fancier appearance.

In either case, you will have the best luck at getting the broom tight if you make a simple device as old as broom-making itself. Using a long rope, tie one end of it securely to something overhead. A stout tree limb or a barn rafter works well. Make a tight loop (not a slip knot) in the bottom so that it clears the ground by six or eight inches and so you can put your foot in the loop (Fig. 13-6).

The broomcorn should still be wet during the tying process, since it not only will be more pliable then but also will expand as it dries. This makes the broom tighter.

To begin the tying, loop the rope once around the broom, between the bottom dowel and the bottom end of the handle. Put your foot in the loop and bear down until the broom is held very tightly. Secure one end of your twine to the bottom dowel, leaving a long "tail" to the knot. Now, wrap the twine several times around the broom as near as you can get to the point where the rope is squeezing it.

Keeping the broom held tight, knot the twine to the tail you left hanging from the dowel. You can remove the temporary ties at this point, leaving the tops of the stalks loose. Pull a few stalks back and run the twine under them to the next dowel. Make a half hitch around the dowel to secure the twine.

Slip the rope up to your next tying point, near the second dowel, and repeat the tying. If you are making a tied broom, continue to move the rope up and make four or five ties about an inch apart, ending at the top of the stalk.

A woven broom takes longer. After the second tie, you begin to wrap the twine in a long spiral, alternating over and under the stalks of broomcorn. To get the twine under, simply pull the stalk back, wind the twine and let the stalk return to its place. If they are thoroughly soaked, the stalks should be pliable enough.

The hardest part of weaving is keeping the twine tight enough. I find this easier if I wind the twine onto a stick, as you would wind a kite string. This is easier to pull tight than a spool or a ball of twine.

When you have woven as much as you think you need (three to four inches for a hearth broom, five to six inches for a floor broom), make several tight wraps around the entire bundle, tie a hard knot and secure the knot to the broom handle with a small upholstery tack driven into the handle of the broom. Be sure this is driven tight.

You can usually pull the stalks together over the tack to cover it. Now trim the stalks off just above this last tie, tapering the tops slightly. Tie a piece of cloth around the sweeps to keep them straight while the broom dries. Trim off any tails of twine.

Trim the bottom of the broom carefully so that it is perfectly even. When it is dry, you may want to touch up the trimming. If perfectly balanced, the handle straight and the trimming even, your broom will stand up by itself! ✶

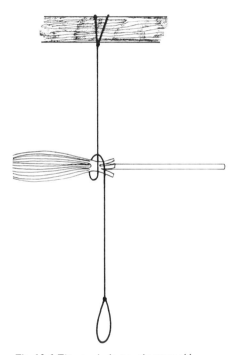

Fig. 13-6 *This simple device, almost as old as brooms, will hold the broom firmly in place for tying.*

CHAPTER

14

Working with Tin

One of the fascinations of antique tinware is its infinite variety. Early pieces vary greatly in design and detail because like patchwork quilts, they were made at home by different craftsmen.

Tin was easy to work with, and utensils could be fashioned from it using only the most common tools. Necessity was the mother of both invention and handicraft for farm families, and often a piece was designed and made to suit a particular purpose, now long forgotten.

So it was with us. We never intended to become tinsmiths. We just wanted to make gingerbread boys. But there were no tin cookie cutters to be found in any store. Plastic ones didn't suit us — the designs were wrong, and they didn't cut well.

Like the farmer of old, we made our own to suit the occasion. Sheet tin was available at our hardware store (it still is at some stores*), and the only tools needed were an electric woodburning pencil with a soldering tip and an old pair of heavy scissors. Tin snips, of course, are made just to cut tin, but we prefer scissors for better control on small work. Tin is as easy to cut as cardboard, and an edge cut with scissors is usually smoother than one cut with tin snips. But use an old pair, as working with tin will dull the best scissors.

Keep the lines in the cookie cutter design simple. Intricate details will be lost or make the cookie dough difficult to remove in one piece.

Draw the design to size (Fig. 14-1) on paper; cut it out and place the cut-out on the tin. Tape down and trace around it with a sharp

*See appendix.

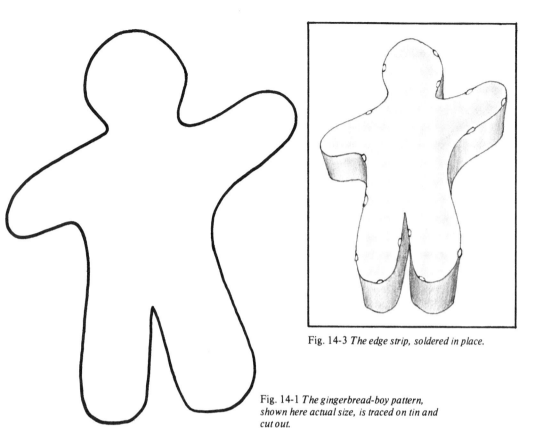

Fig. 14-3 *The edge strip, soldered in place.*

Fig. 14-1 *The gingerbread-boy pattern, shown here actual size, is traced on tin and cut out.*

point — an awl or ice pick works well. Remove the paper and cut the design out of the tin sheet, along the traced line. Flatten the cut tin with a rolling pin to keep the edges from curling.

Measure the outer edge by outlining the entire shape with a piece of string. Cut a straight strip of tin up one edge of the tin sheet, 3/4 inch wide and a little longer than the string (Fig. 14-2).

Beginning at a sharp corner if possible, curve and bend the strip to fit around the flat design (Fig. 14-3). Use pliers for sharp or square corners, or bend the tin over the edge of a table.

For soldering, you will need a small electric soldering iron (or a woodburning pencil with a soldering tip), a few feet of solid wire solder and a can of flux (soldering paste). You can substitute a rod heated over a flame for the electric iron, but the latter is safer and easier for beginners to handle.

Be sure the surfaces are clean and free of fingerprints, which prevent the solder from adhering. A light brushing with very fine steel wool will do this.

Apply flux to the surfaces to be joined and heat by touching with the tip of the iron. Touch the end of the solder wire to the heated surface until the solder melts. By holding the tip of the iron so it touches both surfaces at once, you can melt the solder between them. If this is impossible, melt the solder to one piece and heat the second surface

Fig. 14-2 *A strip the width shown and long enough to go around is cut from the edge of a sheet of tin.*

Working with Tin

while holding the pieces together until a joint of solder is formed between them. Remove the iron, still holding the two pieces of tin together, and wait a few seconds until the solder cools and hardens.

Then you can move on to the next spot. It is not necessary to lay down a solid line of solder, so don't worry if there are small gaps here and there — a cookie cutter isn't meant to hold water! It is tempting to use big spots of solder, but these are no stronger than a thin, even film. It is better to be stingy with the solder and generous with the heat. When the rim is completed, snip off the ends so they meet and solder them together too.

It is possible to make cookie cutters without cutting the design from the tin, by shaping just the rim and soldering it to a square or oblong piece of tin, like a biscuit cutter. This sort of cutter, however, requires a handle, since the edges are not firm enough to get a good grip on when cutting dough. The solid ones are more durable, and it is easier to use a cutter whose exact outline is visible from the top.

After each use of your finished cookie cutters, always wipe them clean. If you must wash them, dry them well (a warm oven is a good place) to prevent rust.

Antique tinware will suggest other projects, such as candle sconces, match holders, Christmas ornaments, and even lanterns or chandeliers. Small items can be made from the flattened sides of food cans. (Cut off the ends of the can, then cut along the side of the can cylinder next to the seam, and flatten the can with a rolling pin. If you are making something round, however, take advantage of the existing curvature and do not flatten the can.)

Fig. 14-4 *A modern Christmas-tree cutter and two antique cutters. The crinkly edges were made by a special machine with matching crimp rollers.*

Fig. 14-5 *Tin cookie cutters designed and made by Stillman Rogers of Richmond, New Hampshire. The church is patterned after the First Church in Keene, New Hampshire.*

Working with Tin

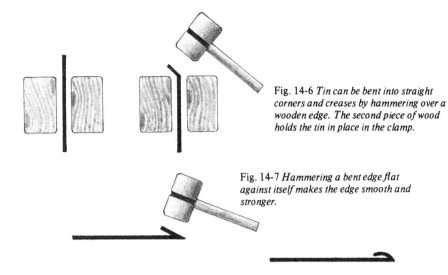

Fig. 14-6 *Tin can be bent into straight corners and creases by hammering over a wooden edge. The second piece of wood holds the tin in place in the clamp.*

Fig. 14-7 *Hammering a bent edge flat against itself makes the edge smooth and stronger.*

Fig. 14-8 *A simple tin match safe or box.*

The sharp edge of the cut tin is needed on cookie cutters, but on other projects, you must fold over a narrow strip along outer edges to seal and smooth as well as strengthen edges. This is like a hem in sewing. Do this "hemming" on strips before soldering in place.

Tinsmiths had a special tool that did this, but you can make a simple device to serve the purpose yourself. Take two hardwood blocks of equal size. Drill matched holes in these blocks so that you can bolt them together with bolts secured with wing nuts to form a clamp (like a tennis racket press without the springs). Place the tin piece or strip between the blocks, allowing only the tin above the fold line to protrude from the top of the clamp. Screw the blocks together tightly to hold the tin firmly. The tin protruding is then either rubbed and pressed down with a hardwood block, or tapped with a wooden mallet, along the fold line to form a straight right-angle bend (see Fig. 14-6). Remove the tin from the clamp and press this right-angle bend over flat, either by tapping with the mallet (Fig. 14-7) or by pinching the "hem" closed with pliers. Wrapping the nose of the pliers with masking tape will prevent scratches and dents.

The edge of a table will also serve to form the right-angle bend in the tin.

The simple clamp described above can also be used to make square corners. Simply bend the tin to a right angle along the fold line and hammer gently until the edge is free of dents.

A match holder is a relatively simple project which uses only two techniques, folding cut raw edges and soldering corners. The design is a box without a lid, or a rectangle with two side flaps (see pattern in Fig. 14-9).

Draw the design to size on paper, cut it out and lay it on the tin. Trace around it with a sharp point and cut the design from the tin. Fold over the three raw edges that form the top opening of the box. The back section should be left rough. Then bend along the fold lines to form an open box. Fold the little soldering lips into place so that they overlap the edges. Fit them to the edges and solder together (Fig. 14-10).

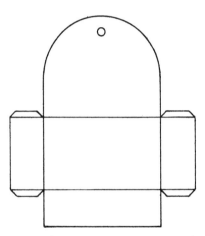

Fig. 14-9 *Enlarge this pattern for the match safe to the desired size. The size you choose will depend on the eventual use of the box.*

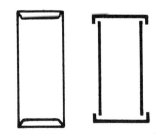

Fig. 14-10 *The edges are bent to form soldering lips and soldered on the outside of the box for strength.*

Working with Tin

97

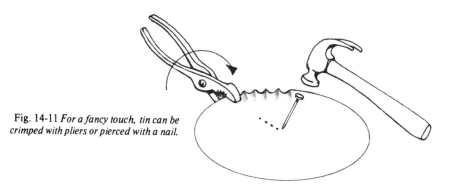

Fig. 14-11 *For a fancy touch, tin can be crimped with pliers or pierced with a nail.*

This flat soldering is much easier than joining two raw edges as you do with the cookie cutters.

The top can be as plain or as fancy as you wish. It can be rounded, cut into an intricate shape, fluted (as you would a piecrust) with pliers, or pierced with a design (Fig. 14-11). In any case, it should have a hole for hanging.

A candle sconce is made in much the same way, with a short cylinder soldered onto the base to hold the candle. A sconce should be taller than a match box and can be narrower at the base. The top of the sconce must be high enough and wide enough to protect the wall on which it hangs from the candle flame (Fig. 14-12).

To make a cylinder, simply roll the tin around an object a little smaller in diameter than you wish the cylinder to be — rolling pin, broom handle, or bottle. The ends of the rolled tin are overlapped and soldered in place.

Piercing tin is a method of decorating which serves a useful purpose. In pie cupboards, pierced tin served as a screen, allowing air circulation while keeping out flies. In lanterns, the piercing allowed light to shine through while the tin shielded the candle flame.

An awl or ice pick, a hammer and a piece of soft board are the only tools needed for piercing tin. Draw your pattern on paper and tape it to the tin. The pattern need only be the outline of the design; it is better to have some leeway as to where the actual holes will go.

Put the tin on the board and punch holes with the awl, following the lines of the pattern. You may need the hammer to assist the awl on its way through the tin. Be careful not to make the holes too close together; closely spaced perforations in the tin tend to break it apart.

The size of the hole is determined by how far you push the awl into the tin. Larger holes are appropriate for a pie safe, but in a small piece, the holes outlining the pattern need only be tiny dents.

If you are replacing tin panels on an old pie safe, it helps to have one surviving panel, even if it is rusted through in places. Put a sheet of paper over the panel and rub with a soft pencil or the side of a crayon. This rubbing will give you the pattern for piercing; the missing bits can easily be filled in freehand.

Lacking an original pattern to copy, you can use any geometric

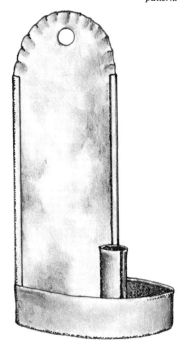

Fig. 14-12 *A candle sconce can be easily adapted from the basic box (match-safe) pattern.*

Working with Tin

Fig. 14-13 *An antique pie safe whose badly rusted tin was restored with new pierced panels by Stillman Rogers.*

design. A diamond with a sunburst in the center (see Fig. 14-13) was a common favorite.

In larger pieces, slits in the tin as well as holes were used to give variety to the design. These slits are easily made with a small chisel and hammer.

The color of the new tin (actually tin-plated sheet iron) is sometimes a concern to those who are restoring an old piece with pierced tin sheets. It is little consolation to point out that the object when new originally was just that color. We are so used to seeing aged tin that the shiny new tin stands out like a neon sign.

Of course, anything you do to dull that shine will hasten the inevitable onset of rust. But if you simply can't abide seeing your own reflection in your pie cupboard, scrub the tin well with steel wool and abrasive cleanser to get rid of the protective coating, and then soak it overnight in a bathtub containing about four inches of water to which two quarts of vinegar have been added.

No matter what you do, the new panel will not look exactly like old tin, but the above procedure will take off the shine.

For cookie cutters or any cooking utensils, leave the surface shiny; the tin will resist rust, be easy to clean, and food will not stick to it badly. For decorative pieces like sconces or match boxes, the shine of the tin is attractive, even if the pieces do look new. Or you can paint the object with flat black enamel and go on to embellish the piece with tole painting, or stenciling. Painting is a boon to the beginner in tin-work, since it helps disguise an uneven **soldering job.** ✹

CHAPTER 15

Marbled Paper

Thought to have originated in 12th-century Japan, the art of decorating paper with designs of swirled color was first introduced to the western world at about the same time as our earliest settlements in the New World. The art was to remain an Oriental and European speciality for some time, but the American Colonists did import these expensive papers for use in bookbinding and other decoration.

Eventually lithographic processes took over the manufacture of marbled papers, but to this day the finest are still made by hand. Yet the craft is easy enough for a child to master, and beautiful results can be obtained by beginners.

The most time-consuming part of the work in early days was preparation of the colored pigments — first pounding them into powder and then mixing the powder with beeswax or ox gall to make a spreadable paint. This paint was tapped onto a surface of gum tragacanth solution, which held the pigment in place. Swirls, stripes and plumed effects were accomplished by dragging a drawing tool through the surface paint to spread and intermingle the colors.

We still use the tragacanth or other sizing solution for more advanced work, but the grinding and mixing is unnecessary now that tubes of oil colors are available. These can be used on plain water for simple swirled effects.

The following initial project is easily managed and can be completed in five minutes. Try this first before attempting more complicated processes.

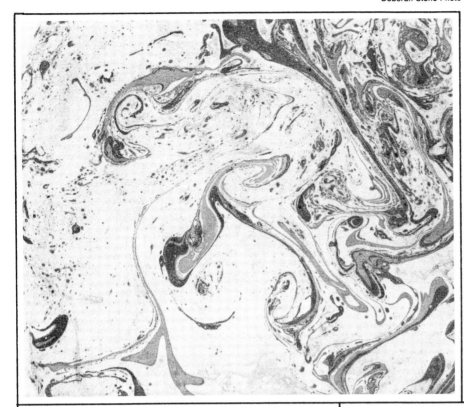

Fig. 15-1 *These marbled papers are by Juliette Rogers of Richmond, New Hampshire.*

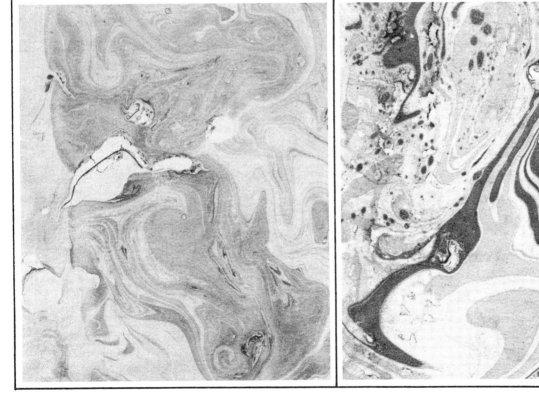

Marbled Paper

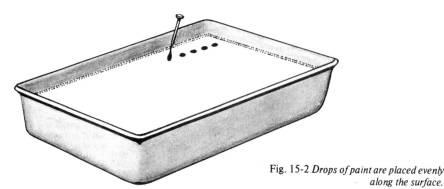

Fig. 15-2 *Drops of paint are placed evenly along the surface.*

Fig. 15-3 *A nail drawn through a row of dots produces a row of hearts.*

Fill an ordinary glass or metal mixing bowl (plastic will be difficult to clean afterward) with lukewarm water to within an inch of the top. In an old jar lid or a piece of foil, drop a dab each of several colors of artists' oil paint. If the paints are not quite runny, thin them with paint thinner (acetone, not turpentine).

With a toothpick, drop a bit of this thinned oil color into the bowl of water. It should spread out quickly over the surface. If it stays in one lump, the paint needs a little more thinning. When it spreads well, add drops of other colors. The normal motion of the water will usually swirl the colors, but if not, stir the surface very gently with a toothpick.

Cut a sheet of plain white typing paper in half and lay one piece on the surface of the water. Try to drop it flat on so that it hits the surface all at once. The corners may stick out, but they can be trimmed later. Wait a few seconds for the paint to be picked up, then remove the paper and place painted-side-up on newspaper to dry.

You have just made your first marbled paper, using the simplest method. The swirls will be random because you cannot stop the motion of the colors on the water. Also, you can do only small pieces of paper at a time in a mixing bowl. But you have the basic method.

To decorate larger sheets, you will need a larger container to provide a greater surface — a rectangular roasting pan, for instance. A glass or enamel drip pan like those that came with old refrigerators works perfectly. The larger the pan, the bigger the pieces of paper you can decorate.

In order to form designs, rather than the purely random swirls of your first experiment, you need to work with a surface more stable than water. The same gum tragacanth that early artists used is still available from artists' supply stores. So is carrageen moss, which is an excellent sizing solution and easier to use than gum tragacanth.

To prepare the size, boil a cup of carrageen moss in two quarts of water for three minutes. Add two cups of cold water and let stand for 24 hours. Strain through a double thickness of old sheet. This size will

Marbled Paper

be good for several days, after which you should prepare a fresh batch.

Thin small amounts of artists' oil colors with thinner as you did for your first experiment. You may print on any matte surface paper (unfortunately shelf paper is too glossy). Most artists' papers and typing papers work well.

Put the moss sizing in the shallow pan and put a piece of newspaper on its surface. Drag this over the sizing once and discard. The surface is now ready to use.

With a nail or small piece of wire, pick up drops of paint and touch them onto the surface of the sizing, where they will spread into circles (Fig. 15-2). By making a series of these and drawing the tip of the nail through them, heart designs can be formed which will stay in place on the size (Fig. 15-3).

The nail can be drawn in parallel lines, swirls or in different directions for a variety of designs. The use of different colors of paint in sequence will also affect the design.

When you have a design you like, hold the paper to be decorated by opposite corners and lower it into the size. Let the center touch first, then let the corners roll down onto the surface to prevent air bubbles from forming. Lift the paper with the design and rinse it under gently running cold water. Or you can blot it lightly with paper towels. Let it dry thoroughly face upward on newspapers.

Repeat the above process with a sheet of newspaper to clear all the leftover paint from the size before beginning another design. As you work with different designs and with different batches of size, you will have interesting variations. Instead of artists' oil, you can try printers' ink or even enamels, although these are not as good. Each will give a somewhat different effect.

You can get some interesting patterns by spattering a small amount of paint in a very light spray using a toothbrush drawn across a stick. A large-tooth comb may be used instead of a nail to make the design known as nonpareil (Fig. 15-4). By swirling the comb slightly to one side you can make the feathery designs so characteristic of early marbled papers.

By constructing your own tool, you can make even more designs. Pound several very thin long nails through a strip of wood at regular intervals about an inch apart, forming a small rake. When this tool is placed on the surface of the paint and drawn in a small circular motion, the beautiful French curl pattern is achieved. Your own experiments will turn up many more designs.

When the papers are thoroughly dry, rub the surface with soap and buff lightly with a soft rag. Store them flat or loosely rolled.

The paper may be used to cover notebooks, boxes, desk accessories, dollhouse walls and many other items. You are limited only by the size of the sheets of paper.

A small project which will give you the feel and technique of working with your paper, but which is so easy a child could complete it, is a letter-clip for organizing letters or papers on a desk.

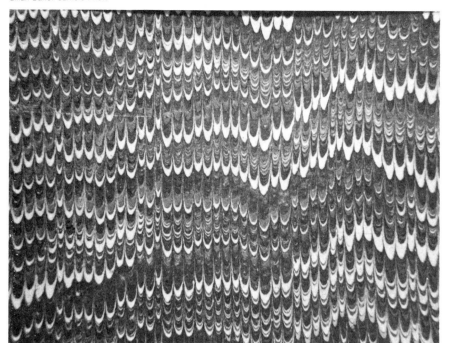

Fig. 15-4 *An example of the nonpareil design that can be created with the aid of a comb. (Courtesy Lilian Baker Carlisle, Burlington, Vermont.)*

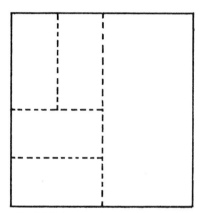

Fig. 15-5 *Cardboard pieces to be covered should always be cut in two directions and laminated together for strength and stability.*

Fig. 15-6 *Assembly of letter-clip from a clothespin, cardboard layers (note reversed grain) and marbled paper.*

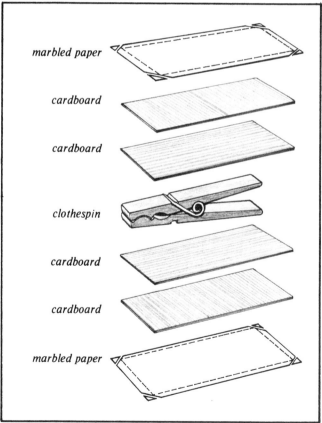

marbled paper

cardboard

cardboard

clothespin

cardboard

cardboard

marbled paper

Begin with a spring-type clothespin. Cut two rectangles of sturdy cardboard (the backs of scratch pads are a good weight) 1/2 inch larger in each direction than the back of the clothespin. Cut two more pieces the exact same size, at right angles to the way you cut the first two (Fig. 15-5).

Glue one of the first pieces to one of the second using white glue; repeat with the other two and put under a book to dry flat. Cardboard has a grain and bends more easily in one direction than the other. By laminating the two pieces with the grain going in different directions, the resulting cardboard is far stronger and will not curl.

Cut two pieces of your marbled paper 3/4 inch larger in each direction than the cardboard. When the laminated cardboard strips are completely dry, lay each on the back of one of the papers, centering it, and mark off a triangle on each corner just 1/8 inch from the corner of the cardboard. This allows you to make a mitred corner that will not be bulky. Cut these corners off (Fig. 15-6).

Thin white glue with water until it will brush easily and cover the entire back of the paper with glue. Center the cardboard again and press. Fold the long sides of the excess paper tightly over the cardboard and press. Very carefully fold over the 1/8-inch excess on the diagonal, pressing it against the edge of the cardboard with your fingernail or a small flat stick. Fold the remaining edges over and press. Allow these to dry.

Using glue that has not been thinned, glue these covered cardboard pieces to either side of the clothespin and again dry thoroughly. These can be made singly or in sets.

The same basic method is followed in covering other flat objects; by adapting it slightly, you can cover books and boxes.

Whatever uses you find for your papers, you can be sure each item you make is the only one like it in the world! ✹

16

Planting a Fragrant Garden

Planning and planting a special garden just for fragrance was a favorite pastime in Victorian days, a delightful custom that deserves revival. In an olitory (the old name for such a garden), plants should be placed so that they are within reach and can be easily brushed by the visitor or gardener because, for many, it is this contact that releases the fragrant oils. Here is an excellent place for a formal garden layout, however small, with paths and borders. A plot ten-foot square will afford plenty of room for an adequate olitory.

Roses, gillyflowers, bergamot, lavender, melissa and the mints, among others, have been cultivated in American gardens since the days of the first settlers, who brought these familiar scents with them from the Old World. Scented geraniums, a fragrant garden stand-by, were a late-comer, reaching a height of popularity during the 19th century, when horticultural historians estimate that there were at least eighty varieties!

Some of the placement of plants will be dictated by fragrance (heavy scents like mignonette could overwhelm delicate herbs like rosemary or lemon balm), and some by the size, height and physical appearance of the plant, including the color of the foliage. Some plants have feathery gray foliage, while the leaves of others are deep green. Consider, too, the blooming season.

Because of their characteristic fragrance and their somewhat unruly habits, the mints might best be either contained in some fashion or planted separately. One possibility is to surround the mint bed with

Fig. 16-1 *Raised beds help improve drainage and impose order in a garden.*

metal edging sunk to a depth of at least a foot. Another is to plant the mint in cement pots which can stand above ground at the corners or ends of the garden.

Some of the mints, such as pineapple, eau-de-cologne and orange, seem easier to contain than spearmint, and it might even be better to use only these fragrant varieties. Corsican mint can be grown between paving stones since its growth is so low, and walking on it will produce a refreshing peppermint odor.

Apart from the mints, most plants can be mingled without too much consideration of their growing habits. Tall plants such as bee balm would be best kept where they won't overshadow others, either visually or literally by cutting off their sunlight.

Because some of the plants have showy flowers and others are primarily foliage, it is wise to think of the appearance of the garden in full bloom and separate showy blossoms by clumps of green.

Whether your fragrant garden is designed to be enjoyed only as a summer garden or also in its dried form in potpourris, sachets and sweet bowls (see page 114 ff.), the choice of plants will be substantially the same

Roses are the basis of most potpourris, and the serious gardener will want the old fragrant varieties for this use. But since growing roses is a subject in itself, it is sufficient here to mention only the most fragrant varieties. These include *Rosa gallica* (French rose), *Rosa damascena* (damask rose) and *Rosa centifolia* (cabbage rose), all old varieties. Modern hybrid varieties, while fragrant when fresh, do not retain their scent when dried.

Because of their size, roses are best grown as borders along fences or walls instead of in a formal garden. If they are used as background for lower plants, they are difficult to reach and their scent cannot be enjoyed as well.

For a rose fragrance in the garden, plant the many varieties of rose geranium. These are the pelargoniums, attractive plants, easy to propagate, and suitable for garden or houseplants. To the potpourri maker, they are invaluable because they retain a true rose scent when dry. Real roses won't do that.

"Clorinda" is one of the best varieties, slightly trailing with attractive flowers, as is "Rober's Lemon Rose," which is larger and heavily scented. One could do with either of these alone, but I've never known anyone who could stop with just one scented geranium. They are like peanuts — you have to have just one more.

Old Spice and Nutmeg as well as Ginger are spicy-scented varieties, and like the rose varieties, hold their fragrance dried. Tomentosum has furry leaves that invite patting and give off a pungent peppermint scent as soon as they are touched.

Lemon, Lime and Prince Rupert varieties have varying citrus scents which, along with lemon verbena, impart a beautiful character to both garden and rose jars.

There are many others, and new varieties join the list each year. One of the newest is Mabel Grey, but this is very difficult to propagate

Fig. 16-2 *Although not as fragrant as their ancestors, dianthus pinks are still a pleasant addition to an olitory. Creeping thyme fills the spaces between the stones.*

Planting a Fragrant Garden

and will probably remain somewhat hard to obtain.

Most pelargoniums, however, are easily propagated and grow rapidly; a few varieties will provide ample scent for enjoyment all summer and for winter drying. Not winter hardy in New England, they can either be potted up in their entirety or be rooted as cuttings and brought indoors for the winter. They are excellent houseplants.

Apart from the pelargoniums, the only true lemon scent that retains its fragrance is lemon verbena. It is a rapid grower, somewhat trailing, with unusual, long tapered leaves. In drying, they curl and provide bulk as well as scent.

Lemon balm *(Melissa officinalis)* is an attractive, upright plant with a lemon oil scent when fresh and a different, but very pleasant scent dried. It is among the earliest recorded plants to arrive in New England; John Winthrop, Jr., ordered it for his garden in the 17th century.

Heliotrope is a low-growing annual with a sweet scent that pervades the air when it is in blossom. It provides bloom in the fragrant garden, adding color from pink to purple.

Lily of the valley is among the earliest to bloom, and a carpet of its white bells scents the evening air around many New England homes. Although it is frequently listed as an ingredient for potpourri, I have never found it to be fragrant when dried. You wouldn't want it in a formal garden, partly because its bloom is gone by the time others are ready to put out and partly because of its invasive nature. A wooded, semi- or completely shaded corner is a good place for it.

The rose is not the only flower to have been hybridized out of its fragrance. The clove gillyflower so often mentioned in old English potpourri recipes was a great favorite, coming to New England with the first colonist and remaining popular through the 19th century. Its strong spicy scent is hardly known today; the new hybrid dianthus varieties are grown instead. Their fainter scent is lost in drying — in fact it fades before the blossom itself. The Cheddar pink is the most fragrant of these fresh, but still does not retain its odor.

The Southernwoods are all gray-foliaged artemesias; the scents vary, but there are lemon and tangerine varieties, as well as camphor. These share the gray, feathery foliage of the other, more common artemesias, but their scent is stronger. Silver mound has a pleasant scent too and grows so beautifully in little clumps that it could form a border for beds.

Bay, rosemary and the thymes are all sweet scented enough to cross the boundary from the culinary garden into the fragrant one. Lemon thyme and silver thyme are the most fragrant and ornamental choices.

The staple herb in the fragrant garden is the stately lavender. Both foliage and flowers are scented, but it is the blossom spike that is dried for the well-known scent found in most potpourris. Spica and Vera are the most fragrant varieties, and will usually winter over in New England. A particularly severe winter may kill plants, but as lavender tends to get woody and straggly after a few years, it is good to replace plants now and then anyway.

Planting a Fragrant Garden

Mignonette is an easily grown annual with a strong, sweet musky fragrance that was very fashionable in Victorian times. It was a window box favorite, not for its flamboyance of bloom but for its fragrance blowing in the window.

For fragrance in the garden which, like the mignonette, does not last when dried, sweet sultan *(Centaurea),* nicotiana, and regal lily are highly scented daytime blooms, and datura will scent your yard all

Plant	Bloom	Scent	Height	Propagation	Notes
Beebalm	showy red, pink, purple or white	foliage, mild	2'-3'	division	
Corsican Mint	none	strong peppermint	1"	division of clump	between stones, needs moisture
Garden Heliotrope (Sweet Rocket)	white	heavy when in bloom	3'	division	tall and spindly
Heliotrope	pink-purple	blossom, sweet and heavy	low	seed	good bedding
Lavender	purple spikes	strong	1'-2'	division	perennial
Lemon Balm	modest	foliage, lemon when brushed	1'-2'	root division, seed	hardy and attractive
Lemon Verbena	none	foliage, lemon when touched	6"-2'	cuttings	not hardy
Lily of the Valley	white	blossom, light and sweet	8"	easily by division	shade
Mignonette	modest	strong in bloom	low	seed	annual
Mints	modest	released on contact	6"-18"	root division	invasive, needs containing
Pinks	fragile and lovely	blossom, clove	1'	division	gray foliage
Rosemary	modest or none	foliage, herbal	1'-4'	cuttings	not hardy: must be in pot
Scented Geraniums	most are modest	varied, released from leaf on contact	varies	cuttings	remain as single, bushy plants — not hardy
Southernwood	inconspicuous	varied foliage	1'-2'	division	gray foliage
Thymes	fragile	leaves, herbal	6"-1'	layering	nice bushy low growth

night with its white trumpets. *Viola odorata,* as you might guess from the name, is a highly fragrant miniature pansy.

Although they are not of notable fragrance, there are two flowers which should be added if the purpose of the garden is to provide material for potpourris. Both add beauty and color to both the garden and the potpourri and both are easily grown. One is the calendula or pot marigold (not to be confused with the French marigold) and the other is the blue cornflower or bachelor's button. They are necessary ingredients for any potpourri that will be shown in a glass container.

Paths for your garden may be turf (a good choice if you are taking up lawn for the beds — just leave paths the width of the mower), crushed gravel, bricks, flat stones or cedar chips.

Herbs don't need good soil, in fact their foliage will have a stronger scent in lean soil. However, the blossoms on flowering plants will be better in good soil. This impossible combination can be achieved by scratching in a little fertilizer around the blooming plants.

All these plants prefer good drainage: only the mints can tolerate wet feet. An attractive way to provide drainage is to raise the beds about six inches, using treated wood, stones, bricks or even poured cement to support them (Fig. 16-1). If the border material is not as attractive as you would like, slightly trailing thymes grown around them will soon cover the border. However, raised beds are not essential, and good drainage should not be a problem unless the area is quite low. A perfect place for a garden is along the top of a stone wall that is used for terracing. The lower level of the earth on the other side maintains drainage and at the same time shows off low-growing plants that grow along the wall.

There are many possible layouts for a garden of this sort. When formal gardens were at their height, many very intricate designs were developed, but for an olitory, where the scent is the first consideration, you will want an easier plan where you can have fun with different varieties and sizes of plants.

I like a square divided into four triangles (Fig. 16-3). It is easy to reach in all areas, looks nice and can be expanded easily if necessary. Another pleasing arrangement is a circle within a square (Fig. 16-4) — unless you plan to have brick paths, since laying circular brick paths is not easy. But with gravel walkways the circle in the square is a beautiful arrangement for the larger garden.

A third design that was well liked in earlier times is called the goosefoot (Fig. 16-5). It resembles a fan, with each bed in the shape of a wedge. It is a good choice if the garden cannot stand alone in the center of a lawn, but must border a house or other building. Goosefoot gardens can be in the form of a half circle against a wall, or a quarter circle if they are in a corner.

Another advantage to this garden is that it does not have to be viewed from all sides. Tall-growing plants like bee balm and garden heliotrope can grow along the back or in the end sections.

The garden shown in Fig. 16-3 can be adapted to a ten-foot square by leaving out one thing in each section — either the center or the

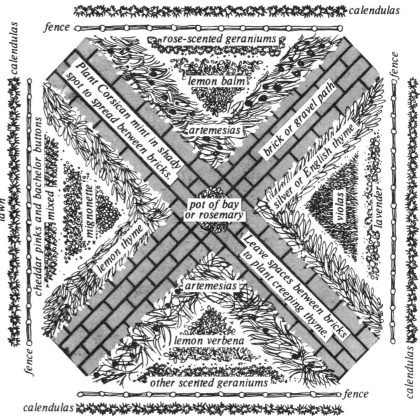

Fig. 16-3 *An X-shaped olitory such as this would fit in a space 10 to 15 feet square. The paths are approximately three double brick rows (Fig. 16-6) wide.*

Fig. 16-4 *The squared circle plan is best suited for a larger area. A circular path should be gravel or stone.*

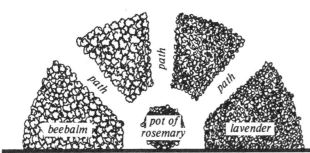

Fig. 16-5 *A semicircular goosefoot garden looks well set against a wall or building.*

planting along the fence. The hedges of artemesias and thymes do give a neater appearance and highlight the shape of the garden, so should be left in.

If the size is ten feet, replace the border of calendulas on the other side of the fence with the planting shown for the back of each triangle. Some of these, such as the scented geraniums, are clumpy plants and don't adapt well to growing in a row, which is why I used the fence and the calendulas when I made this garden at my own home.

With a center bed, you have the luxury of a showy focal point and of corners for other tall bushy plants. The lavender could just as easily highlight the center, with lower plants, perhaps in border rows, used where I've shown lavender. Again, calendulas make a pleasant border and could be used along the outer edges. So could the lavender, instead of being kept in bunches in the corners.

Any of these, especially this latter garden, can be bordered in small shrubs. If you live where they are native, wild bay would provide you with leaves for a lifetime of potpourri. Old-fashioned rose bushes could be grown along a low wall bordering it. This plan is most suitable for a larger garden.

Even a series of borders to existing walkways can provide a fragrant garden.

There are no rules for planting an olitory — merely suggestions. Put your plants wherever you think they will look and smell the best. If a plant grows taller than you had expected, and you don't like its placement, move it. I have plants that must by now feel like gypsies!

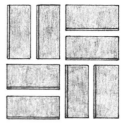

Fig. 16-6 *Paths stay flatter if bricks are laid in opposing pairs on a level base of sand.*

Obtaining the plants or seeds for the fragrant garden can be something of a treasure hunt, but they are available. Some of the perennials are best started with cuttings or rooted plants, since they take several years to raise good-sized plants from seed. A good garden center with a greenhouse may have some of them, but unless a nursery specializes in herbs or scented geraniums, plants are very often mislabeled. I once had a florist tell me in answer to my question, "It's a scented geranium — does it have to be any particular kind?"

Many herb farms also specialize in scented geraniums, and it is best to buy both herbs and geraniums from someone who knows about them so you will be certain of getting the right varieties. Seeds for the annuals are available from the larger seed houses.

Your fragrant garden will reward you well, for there is nothing to cheer the temper and lift the spirits like a slow stroll along a pathway of sweet-smelling herbs and flowers. ✸

Planting a Fragrant Garden

CHAPTER

17

Jars of Summer Scents

The elusive and transient scents of summer's flowers and plants are a seasonal joy. We can delight in them all summer, but in winter they are just a memory. A few pots of scented geraniums can be brought indoors, or a pot of rosemary, but for the most part, garden fragrances last no longer than the summer.

Since the days of great cold gray castles, stale from lack of ventilation and sanitation, people have searched for ways of preserving the fresh smells of herbs and flowers to lighten and sweeten the indoor air.

The heritage of centuries of experimentation comes down to us in an almost infinite variety of sachets, potpourris, rose bowls and other sweet-smelling combinations of dried flowers, herbs and spices. These enjoyed a tremendous resurgence in popularity during the Victorian era, when the scent of lavender was almost a part of a lady's wardrobe.

Receipts for favorite potpourris have come down to us in the faded script of old cookbooks, along with the rules for Grandfather's favorite biscuits. The basic formulae for making potpourris are much the same, but the possibilities for variation are almost endless.

Most potpourris are based on rose petals. These provide the bulk and the foundation scent, which will be modified by the addition of other ingredients.

Not just any rose petal will do. Those of the old-fashioned, highly scented rose varieties keep their fragrance when dried; this is not the

Fig. 17-1 *The potpourri in the glass jar was made from the flowers of a wedding bouquet in 1885 and still retains its fragrance. (Courtesy Mrs. Ewen C. Mac Veagh.)*

case with most hybrid roses. The roses that make the best potpourris are varieties of *R. gallica* (French rose), *R. damascena* (damask rose), *R. alba* (white rose), and *R. centifolia* (cabbage rose), including the apothecary's rose, moss rose, sweetbrier, dog rose and cinnamon rose.

Pick the roses just short of full bloom, as early in the day as possible, but after the dew has dried completely. The petals are then stripped off and laid on screens or pieces of muslin stretched on frames to dry.

Place the screens or frames in an airy place, out of the sun and away from the wind, and leave until the petals have dried. If you put them outdoors, be sure to bring them in at night, or the evening damp will undo the day's drying; you also have to look out for sudden daytime showers. I find my attic to be the best drying area.

Once the petals are crisp and dry, they may be stored in tight-lidded jars until you are ready to use them.

The other ingredients of your potpourri will depend on what you have in your garden. If you grow lavender, dry the flower spikes by hanging them upside down in a dry, dark and airy place. Scented geranium leaves may be dried any time of the year, or whenever the plants are pruned. Simply put them in a pie tin and set over a radiator or on the warming shelf of the stove.

Sweet herbs such as lemon verbena (for a true lemon scent), lemon balm, the mints (apple, orange, and eau de cologne mints are especially prized), camomile, bergamot and woodruff, and some culinary herbs — rosemary, bay, marjoram, and thyme — may be dried by hanging in paper bags in an airy place until ready for use.

Flower blossoms add scent and color to a potpourri, and may be dried on screens or by hanging in clumps. Calendulas, bachelor's buttons, delphiniums, geraniums, and chrysanthemums are all good for drying. Strawflowers and everlastings are often added to commercial

Jars of Summer Scents

Fig. 17-2 *Potpourri and rose bowls (made of dried whole rose buds) are handsomely displayed in any covered glass jar.*

potpourri mixtures as a filler, but they serve no other purpose.

Some of the materials used in potpourris are common kitchen ones. Orange, lemon, and lime peels, stripped of their white inner layer and cut in thin pieces, may be dried in pie tins in the same way as geranium leaves. Other spices such as cinnamon, cloves, coriander, allspice, ginger, anise seed and star anise are stored dry and need no further preparation other than being broken up with a mortar and pestle.

Powdered or ground spices and orris root are fine for potpourris to be stored in ginger or rose jars of porcelain, but tend to give a dusty look to those stored in glass jars.

Essential oils and a preservative increase the useful life of a potpourri. These ingredients must be purchased. Flower or plant essential oils serve to replace those lost in the drying process. They are expensive, but highly concentrated — you need only a few drops. Nor is it necessary to have a wide variety of oils on hand; rose oil alone will suffice for most potpourri needs. The best preservative is orris root, the ground root of the Florentine iris. An alternative preservative is dried sweet woodruff. Woodruff is not as effective as orris root, but you can grow it yourself; moreover, some persons are allergic to orris root, which is a potent sensitizer and should always be handled with caution. Woodruff is also more attractive in a glass jar than the dusty orris root.

Once all the ingredients are ready, mixing can begin. I use half-gallon wide-mouth canning jars to mix in. Since the potpourri requires frequent stirring, the container should have an opening wide enough to let your hand in comfortably. You *can* use a wooden spoon rather than your hand to stir, but half the fun of making potpourris is having the scent linger on your hands afterwards.

The recipes which follow will give an idea of the basic procedures. Variations, combinations and entirely original blends are possible once you have the idea. Like cooking, potpourri making is a process or experimentation to find your own favorites. All the herbs, spices, peels and flowers in these recipes are used dry.

Simple Potpourri

Since this rule uses no essential oil, the potpourri will not last quite as long as those that contain oils, nor is it suitable for sachets. But it is the recipe to start with if you've never made a potpourri before.

2 cups rose petals
1 teaspoon whole cloves
1 teaspoon broken
   cinnamon stick

1 teaspoon whole allspice,
   crushed
1/2 teaspoon mint leaves
1/2 teaspoon orris root

Combine all the ingredients in a covered jar. Stir every few days, mixing well. Ready to use in about ten days.

Rose and Lemon Potpourri

This recipe is good for sachets and for people who do not care for the scent of lavender. This, like the lavender and old rose recipe following, is a classic drawing-room potpourri.

4 cups rose petals
4 cups lemon verbena
2 cups rose geranium leaves
1 cup rosemary
2 tablespoons orris root
1 tablespoon each of orange
    peel and lemon peel

1/4 teaspoon each of
    cinnamon, nutmeg
    and sliced ginger root
6 drops rose oil

Combine the leaves, petals and spices. Sprinkle them with orris and then with rose oil. Stir well. Cover, and stir gently every few days for one month until the scents have blended and mellowed.

Lavender and Old Rose Potpourri

Another classic.

1 cup rose petals
1 cup lavender blossoms
1 cup sweet woodruff
1 cup pot marjoram leaves
    and blossoms (or use
    only 1/4 cup of culinary
    marjoram)
1/2 cup mint

1 tablespoon orange peel
1 tablespoon whole cloves
1 teaspoon crushed
    cinnamon
1 teaspoon orris root
3 drops each of rose and
    lavender oils

Sprinkle the rose and lavender oils and orris root over the other ingredients. Mix well. Cover and stir gently every few days. When well ripened (in about a month), this is excellent for sachets.

Kitchen Potpourri

Keep a small jar of this in your kitchen.

1/2 cup rose petals
(1/4 cup carnation petals)
1 teaspoon each of
    rosemary, marjoram,
    thyme, basil and
    lemon verbena
2 broken bay leaves

1 teaspoon each of anise
    seed and coriander
1/4 teaspoon allspice,
    crushed
1 tablespoon each of lemon
    and tangerine peel
1 tablespoon orris root

Mix well in a jar. Cover the jar, and stir well every few days for two weeks.

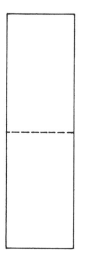

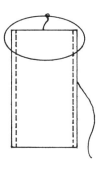

Fig 17-3 *Bathbags and sachets are made in the same way, except that bathbags must have a long loop to hang on the faucet.*

My six-year-old daughter can't read the old receipts, but her nose is unerring. She sniffs the various jars of dried petals and herbs and adds a handful of this and a pinch of that until she is satisfied. It's a little difficult to write down her ingredients, and she will only share her recipes with her pediatrician, but I mention her successes to show that one needn't be limited by other people's recipes.

I am a bit more sharing, and here follows my own favorite spicy potpourri:

Herbitage Farm Spice Potpourri

This rich and spicy blend needs no essential oils added as the spices used in it keep their own oils well. Hibiscus blossoms can be ordered from your herb supplier and do add to the beauty of the mixture, but it is still very attractive without them. Display the potpourri in a glass jar; an apothecary jar or one of the French snap-open canning jars suits its informal nature and shows it off beautifully.

1/2 cup bay leaves
1 cup lemon verbena
1/2 cup marigold blossoms
1/2 cup bachelor's buttons
(1/2 cup hibiscus blossoms)
1/8 cup each of whole
    cloves, coriander,
    cinnamon and allspice

1/4 cup dried orange peel
1/4 cup star anise (a
    Chinese spice)
1/2 cup sweet woodruff

Mix together all ingredients. Cover and stir gently every few days for about a month.

Since the essence of a good potpourri is the proper and subtle blend of scents, only your nose can tell you how to make the best one. Try adding anything that smells good. Save leaves and blossoms from houseplants; you may be surprised to find that they have a pleasant scent. Ginger leaves are an excellent addition, although their color is drab. Some of the headier tropical blossoms — jasmine, hibiscus and orange — can be purchased from your herb supplier.

After your potpourri has been allowed to blend and mellow for the time allotted, you are ready to use it. Simply place the jar in the room you wish scented and remove the cover. The fragrance will spread throughout the room. Be sure to replace the cover between times, keeping the jar closed for at least as much time as it was uncovered. All potpourris need some time to rest and recoup their scents between usings.

Should a potpourri wear out completely, it can be revived quite easily by sprinkling it with more orris root and essential oils and adding a few fresh dried rose petals or spices. Follow the mixing procedure as you would for a new blend. This boost will revive the scents in the old mixture as well as add new material. In this way, a potpourri can often be kept useful for years (Fig. 17-1).

Jars of Summer Scents

Sachets

Sachets can be made from any potpourri, but the most successful are made from those which contain essential oils. The problem with sachets is that they are small and not enclosed in glass or porcelain, so that their scent dissipates rather quickly.

Use at least two tablespoons of your favorite mixture for each sachet. Tie the sachet in a bag made of a sturdy fabric. You need a double-layered bag for sachets containing powdered spices to prevent those spices from sifting out. Spices lightly crushed and broken up with a mortar and pestle are a better choice for use in sachets.

Bathbags

Potpourri mixtures can also be used to perfume your bath with an inimitable spicy scent. Like sachets, bathbags make wonderful gifts. Fill a glass jar with bags of different colors as shown (Fig. 17-4). Run them up from pieces of cotton cloth cut 6 inches by 2-1/2 inches (Fig. 17-3). Fold in half and stitch up the long sides of the bag (1/4 inch seam allowance). Turn and fill with 1/4-1/2 cup of herb mixture. They need not be hemmed. Just tie the necks tightly with string, ribbon or wool, leaving long ends by which to tie the bag on to the hot water tap of the tub. To use, tie to the tap, run the hot water first to extract the fragrant oils at the highest water temperature possible, then let float in the bath while you adjust the temperature of the water and while you bathe.

You can put any herb you like in a bath bag, but certain ones have special properties. Comfrey and houseleek are soothing to the skin. The mints are stimulating (apple, pineapple, orange, and eau de cologne mints are especially fragrant). Yarrow and goldenrod are astringent; peppermint is cooling.

Deborah Stone Photo

Fig. 17-4 *Bathbags in small-patterned fabrics are attractive kept in a glass apothecary jar.*

Herbitage Farm Bath Bag Mixture

1 teaspoon rose petals
1 teaspoon orange blossoms
1 teaspoon dried orange peel
1 teaspoon cut lemon verbena

1 teaspoon camomile
1 teaspoon broken
    cinnamon stick
2 tablespoons oatmeal

Mix well and divide between three bags of cotton fabric.

Other combinations we like are:
Lemon-mint: marjoram, spearmint, orange mint, lemon
    balm, lemon verbena, and dried lemon peel.
Soothing herbs: marjoram, basil, thyme, bay, sage,
    pineapple mint, and comfrey root or leaves.

However you choose to use your potpourri, in sachet, jar or bath bag, you will find its scent a welcome reminder that the seasons do change, that the snow will melt and fresh roses bloom again. ✺

CHAPTER
18

Rose Beads

It is difficult to believe that the natural and elusive fragrance of flowers can be preserved for a century without fading. But rose-petal beads do exactly that. Strings of rose beads generations old will still effuse the delicate and unmistakable scent of fresh roses when they are worn against the warmth of our skin.

The materials are free and the equipment simple. You will need about a half bushel of rose petals. The best kind for fragrance and also the most available are the old "wild" roses — the kind that grow along stone walls and fences and around old cellar holes.

Pick the petals only, or pick up those fresh ones that have fallen to the ground. The petals may be faded, but must be fresh, not dried or brown. Gather about a shopping bag full. This may sound impossible, but if you find an old rose bush, you will be amazed at how fast the picking goes. By picking only the petals, you avoid later sorting and don't interfere with the development of rose hips if the bush is a hip-bearing kind.

You can do as our great grandmothers did and grind the petals to a paste in a mortar and pestle, but it is easier to put them through a hand food grinder. (As soon as Grandmother got a grinder, she did hers that way, too.) The result will be a mass that resembles modeling clay, and your kitchen will smell of roses. Put the ground petals in a cast iron skillet or pot (be sure there's no rust in the pot), and regrind each day for two weeks.

You will see the paste become thicker each day until it reaches a

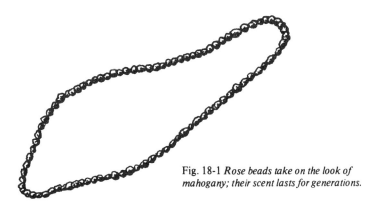

Fig. 18-1 *Rose beads take on the look of mahogany; their scent lasts for generations.*

consistency where it can be formed into smooth, hard beads. To do this, roll little lumps (smaller than marbles) between your hands with a circular motion until they are smooth and well rounded. Put a large common pin through the center of each and stick the pin into a soft board. Continue rolling, piercing and attaching to the soft board (at least 1/2 inch apart) until you have as many beads as you need.

Keep in mind that the finished bead will be half the size of the freshly made one. It will take about sixty for an adult-sized necklace.

Let the beads dry for at least two weeks, longer if the weather is humid. Remove the pins and polish each bead with flannel or other soft cloth. String them on button thread, using a dark color so it will blend with the mahogany tones of the beads. Polish the entire string of beads (which highlights them and is easier than doing each bead).

If the strand is long enough to slip over your head, you will not need a clasp. Otherwise you will need a very plain clasp either from an old necklace or purchased from a craft supply store.

As you wear the beads, they will continue to darken and polish, and release their rosy fragrance. One note for the future. If you store them away, be sure to put a note with them so anyone finding them will know their age and what they are. You may very well be making your great granddaughter's wedding necklace, and you'll want her to know its history! ✳

CHAPTER
19

Making Pomanders

Pleasant scents to perfume one's clothing or stored linens have been popular for centuries, and one of the easiest and most long lasting of sachets can be made from materials available right in your kitchen: fruit and whole cloves.

Pomanders can be made from any of several fruits — apples, crab-apples, pears, oranges, even kumquats. Of all these, I prefer small hard apples. They hold the cloves well, are the least messy to work with and last many years.

There are many suggestions for making the cloves pierce the apple skin more easily, such as first breaking a hole with a pin or nail, but I find that the clove itself is the best thing to use. It makes the skin split to the size and shape of each clove, thus holding them in better and it takes less time.

The object is to cover the apple with whole cloves, leaving a little space (1/8 inch to 1/16 inch) between cloves so the apple can shrink. As it does, the cloves pull together until no apple shows. As you work, apple juice will drip, so work on a table or wear an apron.

When the apple is full of cloves, put it in an open place to dry. Leave it where air can circulate around it for several weeks, or until it is dry and the cloves all touch. Many recipes recommend rolling the pomander in a mixture of cinnamon, cloves and powdered orris root to strengthen and preserve the scent, but I have pomanders that are over ten years old and still going strong without this. The pomander looks considerably prettier without the spice bath.

Fig. 19-1 *A well made pomander dries so that only the cloves show. This one is by Juliette Rogers.*

If you are doing a number of these at once, they are attractive placed loosely in a bowl to dry. They will make a room warm with their spicy fragrance.

When the pomander is thoroughly dry, tie a ribbon or a piece of lace around it. I tie mine on four sides (twice around) and tie a bow on top. A wire hook or string loop may be fastened into the knot for hanging. Gingham ribbons are especially attractive on pomanders, but any ribbon, lace or even rick-rack is suitable.

If you use small fruit, such as kumquats, seckel pears or crabapples, a group of three may be hung on ribbons gathered with a single bow for an attractive and fragrant decoration. Also, a small basket may be filled with these smaller fruit.

Old pomanders may be refreshed by dipping them in hot water and letting them dry thoroughly. ✱

Making Pomanders

CHAPTER 20

Gifts from the Kitchen

Even before the Advent calendar goes up, we know Christmas is coming at our house. The signal is the appearance on the spare table in the dining room of the boxes covered with red brick paper. Each box has a name on it, and as the season progresses, the boxes begin to fill.

At first there are the pickles and jellies saved on a special shelf in the canning cellar. Then the marmalades are added almost as they cool. Next come the tall bottles of Julie's herb vinegars and the jars of our own herb blends.

Bags of herbed rice, sherried pecans, candied orange peel, spiced Brazil nuts, curried pumpkin seeds and horehound drops follow. Fruitcakes, tightly wrapped to ripen, are added a few days before the honey cookies. Just before the joyous day when we load them all into the car to be delivered, we add fresh baked breads, breadsticks, crocks of pâtés and cheese spreads, and decorate the top of each box with little packets of camomile tea and long cinnamon sticks tied with gingham ribbon.

Each box is tailored to the kitchen it will go to. Each goes to good friends, and they've been quick to let us know their favorites over the years. One box will always have an oriental specialty for an accomplished cook with Far-Eastern tastes. Packages of home-grown shallots go to cooks who savor them. Sometimes our baklava is the highlight of a box.

Since we do a number of these gifts, it is important to have as many things as possible that can be done ahead. Some things must be done

Fig. 20-1 *Putting together an assortment of homemade goodies including preserves,* bouquet garni *bags, herb vinegars, and fancy cinnamon sticks is a Christmas project everyone looks forward to.*

in season — chive blossom vinegar, glistening crabapple and mint jellies (chosen for their holiday colors) and our piccalilli and brandied cherries are all done as the ingredients are ripe throughout the growing season.

Dried herb mixtures can be done and packaged any time. Croutons can be cut and dried ahead of time and stored in sealed jars for seasoning and toasting later. Candied orange peel keeps well if sealed in jars.

Fruitcake needs a few weeks to ripen; marmalades are made in November and December when citrus prices are low. Spiced nuts and seeds will keep well for a few weeks. Honey cookies stay fresh for several weeks.

Only the pâtés and breads must be done the very last minute — pâtés the day before and breads the very day of delivery, just cooled enough to be wrapped. If all the scheduling sounds like a countdown, it is a happy one, full of samples to be nibbled, new ideas to be tried, and good smells in the kitchen.

As I mentioned, it all begins with the harvest. There is considerable disagreement over what constitutes "real" mint jelly. I have a friend who disdains jelly made with apple and insists that the only real mint jelly is made with artificial pectin and no apple juice. This seems to me a contradiction in terms, and I like the tart-sweet taste of the apples with the heaviness of mint, so she makes her own mint jelly and I give them something else. Here's how I make mine:

Mint Jelly

Remove stems and blossoms from 3 pounds tart green apples and slice them unpeeled. Add 3 cups water, bring to a boil, covered, and reduce heat to a simmer. Cook 25 minutes and pour, undisturbed, through a jelly bag.

Pour one cup of boiling water over one cup of fresh spearmint leaves, cover and let steep one hour. Drain, reserving the liquid, and press juice from the leaves. To each cup of apple juice, add 3 tablespoons of the mint tea, 1 tablespoon strained lemon juice, and 3/4 cup sugar. Use no more than 4 cups of apple juice for one batch.

Bring to a boil and cook uncovered until the jelly tests done (slides off in a sheet when tipped from a spoon). Add a drop of green food color and pour into sterile jars and seal at once.

Crabapple jelly is, I think, the easiest and most beautiful of all jellies. You never have to worry if it will jell, the color is perfect, and the flavor delicious. Finding the crabapples might well be the most difficult part of it all. If you are fortunate enough to have your own crabapple tree, you will probably want to make spiced whole crabapples, too. Sort out the nearly perfect ones for preserving whole and make jelly of the others.

Crabapple Jelly

Remove stems and blossoms from 3 pounds of crabapples, about one fourth of which are underripe. Cut in pieces and follow directions as above for extracting juice. For each 5 cups of juice, add 4 cups of sugar and boil to the jelly point.

Gifts from the Kitchen

Spiced Whole Crabapples

Run a large needle through 2 quarts of ripe crabapples to prevent skins from bursting. Combine 6 cups sugar, 2 cups white vinegar, 3 cups water, 2 tablespoons whole cloves, 3 sticks of cinnamon, 2 tablespoons whole allspice and a small piece of ginger root and bring to a boil.

Add apples in a single layer and cook over a low heat until they are tender. Remove carefully and repeat with subsequent layers until all the apples are cooked. Add more water if too much boils away.

Pack apples into hot, sterile jars and cover with boiling syrup. Seal and process 10 minutes in boiling water.

I'm hard put to decide which marmalade is my favorite. We make quite a variety of them and whichever jar is open goes on my morning muffins. And it's always, I reflect as I lick the spoon, the one I like best. The one I get the most comments on after Christmas is Pineapple-Grapefruit. It is an interesting combination, and well worth the trouble of peeling and taking the eyes out of the pineapple.

Pineapple-Grapefruit Marmalade

Pare and shred (not chop) one pineapple. Quarter and slice a grapefruit (or two if they are very small) as thinly as possible. Slice a lemon in sliver-thin rings and cut rings in half. Measure the fruit and add an equal amount of cold water. Let stand 8-12 hours in a cool place. Boil gently until the grapefruit rind is tender (take a piece out and bite into it to test it). Allow the cooked fruit to stand another 8-12 hours. Measure again and add an equal amount of sugar. Boil, stirring frequently until it reaches the jelly point. Meanwhile, slice about a dozen maraschino cherries into thin rings. When the marmalade is ready, stir these in and cook, stirring for 5 more minutes. Pour into sterile jars and seal at once. Process for 10 minutes in boiling water.

While any spice or herb mixture made with your own or purchased herbs will be welcome, *bouquet garni* tied up in little muslin bags would be especially useful. Nothing could be easier to make, and you'll want to make up a few extras for yourself. They are much handier than stopping to gather all the ingredients when you are cooking.

Bouquet Garni

Combine in a large bowl one teaspoon each of thyme, marjoram, parsley and savory and 1/2 teaspoon each of oregano and rosemary. Mix thoroughly. Cut five muslin squares (wash fabric well first) about 5 inches across and place on each one 5 peppercorns and a bay leaf. Add one teaspoon of the herb mixture and tie each bag securely with string.

Croutons, lightly herbed and perfectly toasted, can turn an ordinary salad into a masterpiece and a bowl of pea soup into the highlight of a meal. The only trouble in making them is cutting the bread (stale works best) into the little cubes. These are air dried until hard and may be kept in a sealed jar until ready for toasting.

To toast, put a single layer on a cookie sheet, drizzle with a little olive oil and sprinkle with pulverized herbs, such as marjoram, thyme, oregano and savory. For garlic croutons, mash a clove of garlic into the olive oil and let it sit for several days before using.

Put the pan in a hot oven for 5 minutes, remove and turn croutons with a spatula. Continue toasting and stirring, shortening the times between stirrings as the croutons near completion. They do burn very quickly, so I generally do this with the oven door open on the last few stirrings. Cool and seal them in plastic bags.

There are several kinds of spiced and flavored nut and seed snacks that we like, but our favorites are sherried pecans and Brazil nut chips.

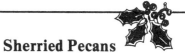

Sherried Pecans

Mix 2/3 cup of brown sugar, 2 tablespoons of sherry and 1 tablespoon white corn syrup in a bowl and add 1-1/2 cups pecan meats. Stir to coat the nuts completely, remove with two forks and roll in granulated sugar, separating the pieces. Let them dry thoroughly on waxed paper and store in sealed containers.

Brazil Nut Chips

Cover shelled Brazil nuts with cold water and bring to a boil. Simmer 4 minutes and drain. Remove any skins that may have adhered and cut nuts in thin chips with a very sharp knife. Spread on a cookie sheet and drizzle with melted butter. Sprinkle lightly with salt and bake 10 minutes at 350°. Stir and bake 10 minutes longer or until lightly toasted. Let them cool before sampling!

Everyone has favorite cookie recipes, but we have one we like for the gift boxes because they keep so well. They remain moist and fresh sealed in plastic bags and can even be used in boxes that are to be mailed some distance. They can also be varied by adding different ingredients.

Honey Cookies

1 cup flour	1/2 cup honey
1 teaspoon baking powder	1/2 cup rolled oats
1/4 teaspoon salt	1/2 cup walnuts
1/2 cup shortening	1/2 cup raisins
1 egg, unbeaten	1 cup chocolate bits
1 teaspoon vanilla	

Beat shortening, honey, egg and vanilla until fluffy. Add sifted dry ingredients and mix well. Add oats, nuts, raisins and chocolate or any combination of these. Drop by teaspoonsful on greased cookie sheets and flatten with a fork. Bake 10 minutes at 375° F. Makes about 5 dozen small cookies.

The day before the gifts are to be delivered is the best time to make pâtés, since they must have time to chill thoroughly. There are many pâtés and meat spreads that make good gifts, but I have chosen this one because it makes such an elegant gift in a crock or any pottery container. This pâté can be presented accompanied only by a bundle of fresh breadsticks tied in Christmas ribbon.

Pâté of Pork

1-1/2 pounds lean pork	1 bay leaf
2 pounds pork fatback	1 shallot
salt and pepper	1 sprig thyme
1/4 teaspoon cinnamon	2 cloves
1/4 teaspoon nutmeg	1 cup boiling water

Dice pork and fat. Tie seasonings in cheesecloth. Add all ingredients to pot. Cook slowly, covered, 2-3 hours, adding water if necessary. Brown toward end. Remove seasonings. Drain, reserve fat. Grind, add salt if necessary. Heat fat and add all but 1 cup to meat. Pack in crocks and cover with reserved fat. Store refrigerated. Serve at room temperature with sour gherkins and pickled onions.

Rye Bread Sticks

1-1/4 cups warm water	3 tablespoons olive oil
1 package dry yeast	2 cups rye flour, unsifted
3 tablespoons sugar	2 cups (approx.) white flour
1/2 teaspoon salt	melted butter
2 tablespoons caraway seed	caraway seed

Combine water, yeast, sugar, salt, caraway and oil in a large bowl. Stir in rye flour and enough white flour to make a stiff dough. Turn onto floured board and knead 10 minutes. Place in a greased bowl, cover and let rise until double.

Punch down, place on board and cut in half. Cut each half into 12 pieces and roll these into long, thin ropes. Place on greased cookie sheets 3 inches apart, cover and let rise until double. Brush with butter and sprinkle with seeds. Bake 15-20 minutes at 400° F. Cool on racks.

Early on the day the gifts are to be delivered, we put the bread to rise. Sometimes it's Italian panetone, other years Russian pumpernickel, but most often it's New England's own anadama, rich-colored and crusty.

Anadama Bread

6 cups unsifted flour
  (approx.)
2-1/2 teaspoons salt
1 cup yellow cornmeal

2 packages dry yeast
1/4 cup soft margarine
2 cups very hot tap water
1/2 cup molasses

Mix dry ingredients, using 2 cups of the flour and add hot water and molasses. Beat at high speed of mixer until well blended. Add 1 cup flour and beat 2 minutes. Add enough flour to make a soft dough. Turn onto board and knead 10 minutes. Place in greased bowl and let rise until double.

Punch down and turn onto board. Cut in half and shape into loaves. Place in greased loaf pans and let rise for half an hour. Bake 30 minutes in a 350° F. oven, or until bread is nicely browned. Remove to racks and brush tops with butter.

The recipe may be doubled. In that case, knead 15 minutes.

Although we present most of our foods in boxes, many of these items make a fine gift singly or in pairs. A loaf of bread and a jar of jam or jelly, for example, is a fine gift in itself. So is a nice fancy jar filled with sherried pecans or Brazil nut chips. A tin of homemade cookies is a perfect gift for a family with children. You know your friends and their tastes, and your own imagination will suggest appropriate gifts for them from your kitchen. ✷

Decorating for an Old-Fashioned Christmas

Certainly no holiday has had such loving and artistic attention lavished upon it as has Christmas. There is no season so alive with tradition, so reminiscent of times, even centuries, past. Things done each Christmas had roots in several eras and many different nations before becoming a part of our own customary celebrations.

In addition, each family has its own holiday traditions, foods and decorations. These are influenced by generations of family, nationality and regional customs. At no time of the year are we more a part of the past — our own and other people's.

The celebration focuses on the home — the hearth, the laden table, the Christmas tree are all part of the warmth that beckons everyone in from the storm to be cheered, fed and comforted.

It is a lovely time of year to decorate a home, rich with tradition, symbolism and memories. Nowhere are these more apparent than on the Christmas tree, the focal point of holiday decorating and the center of every child's interest.

Decorating the tree is an occasion in itself at our house, and each ornament has a story or a memory of the first tree it hung on. In addition, there are the decorations made new each year — the popcorn, the gingerbread boys, the bright frosted cookies.

Although nearly every tree is an "old-fashioned" tree because it has decorations that have been used on others in other years, there are some particular ornaments that have a place in history, since they have graced trees since the days of our ancestors.

Best known are the garlands of popcorn and — in areas where they are available — cranberries.

Easy to make and inexpensive, these garlands have been favorites for many generations and are essential to a traditional tree. They are thought, in fact, to be the first truly American contribution to Christmas decorating. Freshly made popcorn, unbuttered and unsalted, works best. (We make two batches — one to string and one to eat.) Use a double thread as long as you can handle without tangling and a long regular sewing needle. Choose large puffy pieces of popcorn and put the needle through slightly into one side of the kernel. This helps to avoid broken pieces, although some will break no matter how careful you are. Leave a little thread at each end and tie the strings together into long garlands before hanging.

Cranberry garlands, also dating from Colonial days, are even easier to string, again on a heavy double thread. They don't break when strung, but do be prepared to have a little juice dripping in your lap.

Many people alternate popcorn and cranberries on the same string, but since we have our tree up for a long time, I find that the juice from the berries ruins the popcorn in a few days, spoiling the whole string. We also love the strings of bright, shiny berries all by themselves.

Popcorn and cranberries can also be strung on stout wire and used with sprays of Christmas greens in a vase, much as you would use bittersweet.

Along with popcorn and cranberries go the traditional gingerbread boys (and girls). We make these in great number each year and embed wire hooks before baking in the tops of those we plan to hang. Any rolled spice cookie recipe will do, but we have found it wise to add a little extra flour to the dough to make the cookies slightly tougher and more sturdy. You can use frosting to decorate them, but we prefer to push currants into the unbaked cookies, since frosting lines tend to fall off as the gingerbread boys are handled.

Gingerbread Boys

1/2 cup molasses	1/2 teaspoon baking soda
1/4 cup sugar	1/2 teaspoon salt
3 tablespoons shortening	1/2 teaspoon each, cloves
1 tablespoon milk	ginger and cinnamon
2-1/4 cups flour	

Heat the molasses to boiling and add the sugar, shortening and milk. Sift the dry ingredients together and add. Chill the dough one hour. Roll out and cut. Bake 8-10 minutes at 375° F. on greased cookie sheets. Press currants in for features before baking, if desired, or frost with white icing.

Along with gingerbread boys, we make a variety of sugar cookies cut in traditional shapes — Christmas tree, stocking, boot, wreath,

Fig. 21-1 *Decorated sugar cookies make colorful tree ornaments.*

bells, snowmen — and decorated with colorful frostings. Some of our cookie cutters are very old, some of our own manufacture (see page 94).

Again, any rolled sugar cookie recipe will do, but a little extra flour makes them more durable. Hooks are embedded before baking, and the entire cookie is covered with frosting when cool. Decorations are added and lines drawn on with a pastry tube while the coating of frosting is still fresh, so they will adhere better.

Rolled Sugar Cookies

1/2 cup butter	1 tablespoon milk
3/4 cup sugar	1-1/2 cups flour
1 egg	1/4 teaspoon salt
1/2 teaspoon vanilla	1/4 teaspoon baking powder

Cream the butter and sugar. Add the egg and vanilla, beating well. Add the milk and dry ingredients sifted together. Chill the dough one hour. Roll and cut. Bake on ungreased pans about 8 minutes at 375° F.

Cookie Frosting

1/4 cup butter
1/4 cup milk
confectioners' sugar

Melt the butter, add the milk and beat in enough sugar to give spreading consistency. Flavor with vanilla if desired, and color with food coloring.

Carved wooden ornaments, once plentiful and inexpensive, are now very expensive and not too easy to find. But we have another tra-

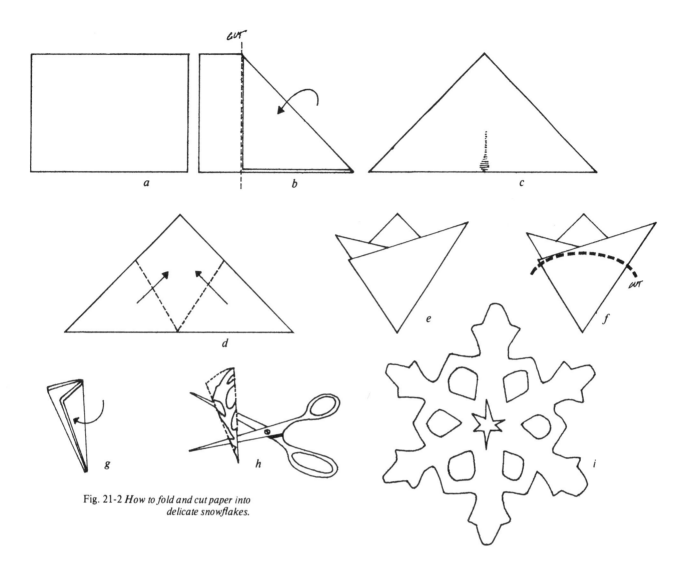

Fig. 21-2 *How to fold and cut paper into delicate snowflakes.*

dition which provides us with a variety of these. Each year, when we take down our tree, we cut a piece of it off, label it, and set it on the mantel to dry.

Sometime during the year, this piece of wood is carved into an ornament and carefully marked on the bottom with the year. We have a snowman, a sled, a bugle, a violin, a pine tree, and many others. In this way, each tree becomes a permanent part of our Christmas.

There are other traditional decorations, too, such as cornhusk dolls made with the husks of our first harvest on the farm (see p. 11), and the cut-paper snowflakes we made during a Christmas blizzard. Snowflakes are quickly made and can be as intricate or as simple as you wish. You'll need small, sharp scissors and white paper — not too heavyweight. Inexpensive typing paper is about the right weight.

Cut a sheet of paper square. For the tree, you will want to make your snowflakes from squares as small as 1-1½ inches a side. But if

Fig. 21-3 *Paper snowflakes will flutter in the slightest draught.*

Deborah Stone Photo

Decorating for an Old-Fashioned Christmas

135

Fig. 21-4 *Tiny cornhusk dolls enhance a traditional tree.*

Fig. 21-5 *Hang paper figures in old-fashioned costumes amid garlands of popcorn and cranberries.*

you have never cut a snowflake before, experiment first with larger squares, measuring six or eight inches a side. Fold the square in half diagonally (Fig. 21-2a,b). Bring the two bases of the triangle so formed together just enough to form a small crease in the center (Fig. 21-2c). Using this crease as the center point, fold the triangle into thirds (Fig. 21-2d,e). Trim from points A to B in an arc (Fig. 21-2f). Fold in half once again (Fig. 21-2g). This not only gives you a six-pointed star, it gives you as many layers as you can cut neatly.

Make random snips, cutting holes of different shapes, taking care not to cut at any time all the way across the wedge (Fig. 21-2h). Snip a little shape out of the tip of the wedge. The more deeply you cut the outer edge, the more pointed your snowflake will be, and the more like a real one (Fig. 21-2i).

When there is no more place to snip, unfold carefully and press flat with a warm iron. Tie your snowflakes to the tree with dark thread, and let them hang free where the slightest breeze will make them flutter (Fig. 21-3).

Among our most treasured decorations are a set of paper figures dating from the turn of the century. Hard as I've tried, I have never been able to duplicate their perfection, but I have at least been able to figure out how they are made and adapt them to modern materials.

They are only two or three inches tall and are formed over a wire skeleton. I find that very narrow strips of crepe paper work well for wrapping the frame. Use a flesh-colored paper and cut it in 1/8-inch strips. If wound tightly and stretched slightly as wound, this makes a smooth surface, even in rounded areas like the chin. Keep wrapping until the body is well shaped, securing ends with a drop of glue.

The dolls may be dressed with crepe or tissue paper, or even bits of lace. Ours are a group of carolers from Dickens' time, a Santa and Mrs. Santa, but any figures, including the Nativity group, could be made (Fig. 21-5).

The beauty of most of the old Christmas ornaments is that they were handmade, and so they can be duplicated today. If you can find examples of these old decorations, or even pictures of them, you can probably figure out how they were done.

Cornucopias full of hard candy were popular on Victorian trees and are easily made from heavy construction paper. Cut out a large circle of paper and cut it in half. Roll into cones and tape or glue securely. Make a hole for hanging in the double portion where the seam is. These can be decorated around the inside of the rim with paper doilies, as their Victorian ancestors were, or left plain and filled with hard candy and candy canes.

Little baskets may be used instead of cornucopias; they can be filled either with candy or with tiny dried flowers, sprigs of evergreen or bittersweet.

Larger baskets of evergreens can carry this theme throughout the house. Popular in 17th-century England, the use of evergreen boughs began with the Romans and was later adopted by the Christians. Along with pines, holly and mistletoe, the herbs rosemary and bay

Decorating for an Old-Fashioned Christmas

were frequently used.

Evergreen plants are the symbol of immortality, and the Colonists found many new ones in the winter woods. Along with the greens, rosehips, alderberries and bittersweet add a lively contrast. Sprays of these can be placed in vases or bowls, but we like to combine them in natural baskets. (Alderberries are the fruit of the alder tree.)

Fruit motifs joined the Christmas decorating in 18th-century Europe where della Robbia wreaths were popular. In America the terra cotta wreaths were replaced with evergreens and real fruits.

Fruits and greens are perfect in a dining room, where a low fruit basket with sprays of white pine tucked between the fruit makes a centerpiece. We use fruit alone to fill a large hurricane lantern globe. Around the base of this pillar of fruit is a wreath of greens.

Fruits and greens go nicely with candles, and we often surround our brass candlesticks with small evergreen wreaths. A tall centerpiece for a buffet or side table can be formed on a cone of wire. Use chicken-wire fencing to form a cone and fill it with sprays of white pine to form a Christmas tree. Impale bright red apples or crabapples on long wooden skewers and push the skewers into the tree among the pine sprays (Fig. 21-6).

Fig. 21-6 *A centerpiece of pine sprigs and apples on a chicken-wire cone.*

Many other traditional crafts have been adapted to Christmas decoration. The crèche, whose origin is credited to St. Francis of Assisi, can be made of cornhusk dolls. Apple-head dolls (see page 24) can be a part of many Christmas decorations, and are particularly attractive in a mantelpiece arrangement. Pomanders (page 122), piled in small baskets, are a beautiful and fragrant addition to any room.

"New" traditions are born each year and join those of other years and other centuries. At our house, we define a Christmas tradition as anything we did during the holidays that we enjoyed. And somehow, even in a house already filled with greens and candies and good things to eat, there's always room for a new tradition or two. ✸

Appendix

Some Sources and Additional Reading

Here are some suggestions as to where to look for the materials used in the various projects of this book. Where particular sources are mentioned, they are those I have used myself, but by no means the only ones. I mention them only in the event that you cannot find what is needed in your own area.

Similarly, there are excellent books out on many skills described. I mention here only those that I have used and found of particular value.

Bayberry Candles: Candle wicking and molds are available at most craft supply stores or from — American Handicrafts, P.O. Box 2911, Fort Worth, TX 76101

Rug Braiding: Arthur Wicks, 106 Spanish Oak Drive, RD 2, Myrtle Beach, South Carolina 29577.
Braid-Aids are available at most needlework shops, or may be purchased from — Braid-Aid, 466 Washington St., Pembroke, MA 02359
How to Make Braided Rugs by Sally Clarke Carty, McGraw-Hill, N.Y., 1977, has excellent directions for other and more complicated rugs.

Bronze Stenciling: Architect's linen is available at stationery stores, and bronze powders can be purchased from craft suppliers. All stenciling supplies can be ordered from — Arthur Brown and Bro., Inc., 2 West 46th St., New York, NY 10036.
A full range of high quality artists' brushes and oil paints is carried by — Utrecht Linens, 33 Thirty-fifth St., Brooklyn, NY 11232

Theorem Painting: See above for sources of stenciling supplies, oil paints and brushes.

Patchwork and Quilting: Sears, Roebuck Co., carries quilt batting, frames, etc., as does Herrschners (see Cross-Stitch Samplers, below). A large variety of different battings can be obtained from —
Taylor Bedding Mfg. Co., P.O. Box 979, Taylor, TX 76574

Cross-Stitch Samplers: Hardanger and Aïda fabrics for counted-stitch embroidery are carried by —
Herrschners, Inc., Hoover Road, Stevens Point, WI 54481
Hoops, thread, embroidery needles, etc. can be purchased in sewing departments (of large stores) and needlework shops.

Swedish Weaving: Pamphlets, patterns and huck toweling can be found at —
The Huckery, P.O. Box 59, 290 Hempstead Ave., Malverne, NY 11565.
Huck towelling is also sold by Herrschners, Inc. (see Cross-Stitch Samplers, above).

False Graining, etc.: Materials and supplies for these procedures are found in paint stores and artists' supply shops.

Broom Making: Broomcorn seed may be obtained from —
Gurney Seed and Nursery Co., Yankton, SD 57079

Working with Tin: Sheet tin is available at hardware stores. In New England, the Aubuchon Hardware chain carries it.

Marbled Paper: Bookcraft, Box 6048, Hamden, CT 06517 has marbling moss, papers and other supplies. Talas, 104 Fifth Avenue, New York, NY 10011 also has moss.
An excellent reference work on marbled and other decorated papers is —
Decorative Papers and Fabrics by Annette Hollander, Van Nostrand Reinhold Co., New York, 1971.

Fragrant Garden: Seeds are available from most seed houses, and plants may be purchased from nurseries. Some of the hard-to-find plants are best sought at herb nurseries. Three excellent herb nurseries are —
Nuthatch House, Hopkinton, New Hamp-

shire (RFD 1, Concord, NH 03301); Stonehenge Gardens, Charlton, MA 01507; and Treehouse Workshop, Goffstown, NH 03045. The latter two will not ship plants, but both are worth a visit.

Potpourri: Herbs, spices and oils for potpourris are available from —
Pickety Place, Nutting Hill Road, Mason, NH 03048
(Pickety Place will send you a catalog on request.)
And also from —
Mother's General Store, Box 506, Flat Rock, NC 28731

Gifts from the Kitchen: Recipes for unusual and traditional canning and preserving can be found in —
The Pleasures of Preserving and Pickling by Jeanne Lesem, Alfred A. Knopf, New York, 1975.
The Forgotten Art of Making Old-Fashioned Jellies, Jams, Preserves, Conserves, Marmalades, Butters, Honeys and Leathers, Yankee, Inc., Dublin, New Hampshire, 1977.
The Forgotten Art of Making Old-Fashioned Pickles, Relishes, Chutneys, Sauces and Catsups, Mincemeats, Beverages and Syrups, Yankee, Inc., Dublin, New Hampshire, 1978.